HALFWAY TO DIFFERENT

A BICYCLE ADVENTURE

J.P. TUTHILL, SR.

Gotham Books

30 N Gould St.
Ste. 20820, Sheridan, WY 82801
https://gothambooksinc.com/

Phone: 1 (307) 464-7800

© 2023 *J.P. Tuthill Sr.* All rights reserved.

No part of this book may be reproduced, stored in a retrieval system, or transmitted by any means without the written permission of the author.

Published by Gotham Books (September 01, 2023)

ISBN: **979-8-88775-390-4** (P)
ISBN: **979-8-88775-391-1** (E)

Because of the dynamic nature of the Internet, any web addresses or links contained in this book may have changed since publication and may no longer be valid.

The views expressed in this work are solely those of the author and do not necessarily reflect the views of the publisher, and the publisher hereby disclaims any responsibility for them.

ACKNOWLEDGEMENTS

To John for making
the trip possible.

To JP for being born as my
one and only son.

FOREWORD

Halfway to different recounts my 1979 bicycle trip on the TransAmerica bike route from Richmond, Virginia to Pittsburgh, Kansas, hence the reference to going halfway. By pedaling through four and into five of the ten states that make up the old Bikecentennial trail, I learned a lot about life and living on the road. I found a single commonality cycling across country back in 79, Americans were generally quite friendly toward strangers, or so was much of my people encounters. However, I am not sure a similar claim could be made now in the 21st Century, but I like to think so. The chemistry of cyclists, enthusiasts and small-town residents has hopefully gone unchanged through the passage of time.

Certainly, people continue to make the TransAm bike trek every year and doubtless this summer as well and I hope that people and places that cyclists meet along their journey are enriching as those I pedaled into back in 79. There is no better way to see the country and experience attitudes of everyday Americans than touring the USA on the saddle of a ten-speed bicycle. I faithfully maintained a journal of my trip, which I suspect some cyclists do to document their adventures and this book recounts my journal in nine chapters with an Epilogue.

The title of my book came to me while recalling my reason for making the bicycle trip. There were several purposes of motivation for making this journey, but to simplify, which is a trait I commonly exercise, I lumped them altogether into a single incentive, being different. Since I cycled approximately half of the trip, some eight-teen hundred miles before returning home, I came up with the title; Halfway to Different. The best part of my bicycle trip was seeing the country's landscapes surrounding small town America and meeting some of the people who live there, as well as fellow cyclists.

The worst part was finding places to sleep after a full day of pedaling through mountain backroads. Some of the suggested places to stay and make camp no longer existed three summers past the initiation of the Bikecentennial trail in 1976. The maps and accompanying trail guides came from Adventure Cycling Association (ACA) in Missoula,

Montana for the Bikecentennial tour and by 1979 some of the suggested campsites had vanished from reality.

It was a bit frustrating to arrive at the end of the day after excruciating climbs up hilly, mountainous terrain to find a designated place to sleep was no longer there. Or find roads along your route that were closed as the maps and guides had not been updated. In the pre-Internet and GPS tech days, we relied on the printed map and travel guidelines to navigate our path. When we could not find an ACA, or Bikecentennial recommended campsite, we asked locals for suggestions for accommodations. Like Blanche Dubois in A Streetcar Named Desire we occasionally depended on the kindness of strangers. Surprisingly, that kindness sometimes came in the form of a free meal, or place to stay.

We slept in churches, churchyards, as guests in homes, abandoned homes and even graveyards. I like to jest in reminiscing that bike trip that I slept everyplace, but a jail, which is hardly an exaggeration. Equipped with a descent sleeping bag, Optimus backpacking camp stove and a Coleman lantern, I could pretty much eat and sleep anywhere.

My journal entries that were made from June 11 to July 20, 1979, are duplicated in the text of this book and the epilogue captures a look back at my bicycle adventure some forty years later. Any ambition I had to complete the cross-country trek from Kansas to Oregon is long gone, faded beneath the objectives to provide for my family and raise my son the best I could. Now, those objectives also fade in my retirement and pass into memory of where I have lived and loved in life. Since then, I have taken residence in Amity Harbor, NY, Nashua, New Hampshire, San Jose, California, Okinawa, Japan, Hacienda Heights, California and Mesa, Arizona.

In my obesity and my retirement, the chances of completing the cross-country bicycle trip have become even more remote. In retrospect, I have no regrets. I am glad that I made the trip as far as I did. I am glad I was able to document my adventure in this book and I hope you enjoy reading the story.

TABLE OF CONTENTS

CHAPTER I 1

THE PREPARATION

CHAPTER II 7

AT THE START

CHAPTER III 18

LEAVING VIRGINIA

CHAPTER IV 25

PASSAGE THROUGH THE BLUEGRASS STATE

CHAPTER V 34

NEW MONTH IN KENTUCKY

CHAPTER VI 43

OVER THE RIVER TO ILLINOIS

CHAPTER VII 52

ACROSS THE BIG MUDDY IN MISSOURI

CHAPTER VIII 59

FINISHING OFF THE OZARKS

CHAPTER IX **67**

GOING HOME

EPILOGUE…..……………………………………………...**72**

CHAPTER I

The Preparation

John and I began our bicycle trip in Richmond, Virginia and took the Amtrak train from Penn Station to Richmond in early June of 1979. Many years have passed since we took our great adventure on the Bikecentennial Tour, yet I'll accurately recount the trek from the journal I kept during our excursion. I grew up around the block from John in the small suburban town of Amityville, NY. Amityville is in the middle of Long Island in Suffolk County that borders Massapequa in Nassau County to the west with South Oster Bay lapping at her coast.

I liked growing up in Amityville, a village town with a village police force that kept crime at a minimum. However, at twenty-three I was itching to leave and see what life was like in other parts of the country. I got a taste of new environments having lived in Richmond, Virginia for a year in 1977-78, which made me hungry for more travel and to experience new adventures.

Our little town became famous, or more accurately infamous, with the DeFeo murders of 1974 that were later hyped into a series of books and movies known as the Amityville Horror. In the early morning hours of November 13, 1974, Ronald DeFeo Jr. shot and killed six members of his family at 112 Ocean Avenue, a large Dutch Colonial house situated in a suburban neighborhood in Amityville, on the south shore of Long Island, New York. He was convicted of second-degree murder in November 1975 and sentenced to six terms of 25 years to life in prison.

In December 1975, George, and Kathy Lutz and their three children moved into the DeFeo house. After 28 days, the Lutzes fled the house, claiming to have been terrorized by paranormal phenomena while living there. Subsequently, the book, "THE AMITYVILLE HORROR, A True Story" written by Jay Anson was published in 1977. A series of films followed the bestselling fiction, which put Amityville back on the list of places to visit and see the infamous house. The Friendly Village by the Bay became less friendly and shunned all publicity regarding the Amityville house. They even denied all films about the supposed possessed house to be filmed there, starting with the first released movie in 1979 and the 25 that followed.

I should have realized the effect of Anson's concocted paranormal, bestselling phenomena would have on our peaceful little town. It should have been crystal clear to me when people starting showing up in Checker Cabs from NYC asking for directions to the Amityville Horror house. Now, I am not saying that the Amityville Horror, which Anson touted as being a true story is in fact true, or hoax. It seems the house on Ocean Avenue in Amityville was investigated by paranormal researchers and arguments have been made on both sides.

What I do know is that the book and subsequent movie thrust our peaceful little town under the public's magnifying glass. Anything held under a magnifier for too long will eventually wither and shrivel to the point of becoming a crisp shell of its former self. The tourists began showing up in droves to see the house on Ocean Avenue made demonically infamous by published book and popular movie. Subsequent to the dark wave of publicity, Amityville grew into this place known throughout the country and probably a good part of the world as a town of horror.

Who profited from all the publicity? Someone always profits from publicity, good or bad and in this case, it was certainly bad for Amityville, but who made the profits? Well, Jay Anson certainly did as the author of a best seller, those who created the film from the book did I'm sure and the Lutz family probably did as well. However, no one else from our town profited. The Village Board shunned all publicity and would not allow the movie to be filmed at the actual house location. So, a similar house somewhere in New Jersey was found to make the movie. Most of the townsfolk saw the entire escapade as a blemish on our tranquil village. This was my mindset back in the late seventies and whenever a car pulled over to ask me directions for the Amityville Horror house, I would direct them out of town, maybe to Amity Harbor, or Copiague.

One of the tee-shirts I wore on my bicycle trip was artistically crafted by my girlfriend, Patti and featured NEW YORK painted boldly on the back and front. Whenever anyone saw me wearing that shirt, they would ask where in New York I was from and when I answered Amityville, they instantly knew of the town. Fame from the Amityville Horror preceded John and I on our bicycle trek across country. We did not benefit from this recognition, we merely cycled along and to some, I am positive, as a curiosity, as being different, coming from a place where there was an infamous haunted house.

I look back on that situation in the town of my birth these forty plus years later and wonder if they could have used the publicity to their advantage? Rather than shunning the tourists, the curious and the moviemakers, the town should have purchased the house, hauled it down to the public beach and charged admission to tour the Amityville Horror. Instead of making tee-shirts that read **Amityville Is No Horror**, they should have advertised the Hell out of the house with a genuine paranormal presence.

Maybe the town should have embraced the notion of a haunted house with a massive marketing campaign, like an attraction in Disneyworld. If they welcomed tourism to the Amityville Horror, instead of doing their utmost to ignore and dissuade, they may have paid off the town budget for a decade or more. Amityville could have changed from the friendly village to the friendly ghost village. This may have been a missed opportunity and maybe it wasn't, but if you are made famous, even by some tragedy, you should at least try to get paid for the trouble.

I lived in Richmond, Virginia for one year prior to 1979 and when John proposed the trip to me, I remember that I jumped at the chance. I am not sure how John discovered this cross-country bicycle trip, but during the winter of 1979 he showed me an Ad for the Bikecentennial tour, established first in the summer of 1976. Bikecentennial is still around, now called Adventure Cycling and they opened the door to long distance travel by bicycle in the bicentennial year from their headquarters in Missoula, Montana. I chipped in with John to purchase the TransAmerica trail maps and accompanying guidebooks, and we began to plan our trip.

Prior to the arrival of Spring thaw, I purchased a new ten-speed touring bicycle. I bought a Schwinn Superior and outfitted her with a

Brookes leather saddle, a rack over the rear tire, Bellwether rear panniers, Zefal high-pressure bicycle pump, water bottle and bike mounted holder, and a blue, Cannondale handlebar bag. I recall my Schwinn looking quite elegant with blue, steel, double-butted frame, the Zefal pump and water bottle mounted to it, the silver Cannondale rack in the rear and the handlebar mounted bag. I packed forty-five pounds of goods into my panniers and secured them to the Cannondale rack. With the added weight, my bicycle weighed approximately seventy-five pounds and I worried if I could pedal that load across the country.

By March John and I had passed from the planning to the training phase of our adventure yet found ourselves in an unchallenging and disadvantaged location to prepare for a cross-country bike trip ... the flatness of Long Island. Each weekend we would bicycle from Amityville to Jones Beach State Park in Wantagh and back, traveling west along Montauk Highway. As the day trip to the beach, like most cycling on the island, gave us flat sometimes rolling terrain, we knew our training was ill preparation for the mountain climbs foreseen on our adventure. We even undertook one or two overnighters to Montauk Point, approximately 100 miles from our hometown, which sharpened our endurance, but did little to prepare us for mountain biking.

The twelve regional maps and camping guidebooks finally arrived from Bikecentennial, so John and I studied them each evening, and planned to set out from Richmond, Virginia in June. We had a place to stay in Richmond, a house where I had resided for a year in 77 and 78. My former residence was a rented house on Three Chopt Road, sitting on approximately five acres of land. This would serve as respite for a day, or two, while we reassembled our bicycles to begin our journey. As our departure date grew near, we increased our exercise trips to Jones Beach State Park and strategized to ease the weight burden while on route. John came up with a brilliant solution for this concern, he mailed care packages containing food to himself at various post offices along the route to minimize what we needed to carry in our panniers. We also brought money to make purchases, buy food and pay for campsites, etc., so I saved up to carry with me $700.00.

Sometime before John told me of the Bikecentennial trip, my girlfriend, Patti informed me that she was pregnant. Patti and I decided that neither of us were ready to raise a child, and later I committed to the bicycle adventure with John. The both of us agreed not to wed at that time, arrange for our child to be adopted and the adoption agency would pay the expenses. Of course, Patti would not be allowed to hold her child after delivery, and I would go before a Judge to declare myself a knowingly negligent father. I have been put in a degrading position at least once where my spirit was diminished to some degree. Yet, on that occasion in municipal court was most probably the worst in my life. Standing before the Judge and Court Stenographer with pregnant Patti by my side, as the acts of my negligence were read off for me to acknowledge filled me with a craven disgust of myself.

Upon admitting my negligence and signing a statement the Adoption Agency agreed to pay for the delivery of our child. It is not an easy thing to do signing away your first born and looking forward to spending the rest of your days wondering what he, or she will grow up to be like. Will they look like you? Will they have any of your mannerisms? Will they do better in their life than you did? These are the things that ran through my head as I stood before the court, belittled by the proclamation of my negligence to arrange for child adoption.

Patti and I agreed that we would maintain our relationship despite giving away our first-born child and I promised marriage after completing the cross-country bicycle adventure. I planned bicycling down the coast to California after reaching the end of the trip in Astoria, Oregon. There I would set up a new life with a job and a place to live and send for Patti to join me. Not much of a plan … more like a fanciful desire and a culmination of my adventure. My beloved and pregnant girlfriend agreed to this shallow plan, but first I must legally declare my negligence in abandoning my unborn child to make the NY State supported adoption possible. I must live a nightmare to realize my dream.

Our friends threw a party for John and I using the Amityville bowling alley bar as the venue a few nights before our departure. I recorded several friends' names and addresses in the newly acquired journal before getting blind drunk only to stumble home with Patti. For the trip I also purchased padded cycling shorts, cycling jersey with back pouch, fingerless bicycle gloves, cycling helmet and bicycle shoes. John acquired two sleeveless safety vests in yellow with orange triangles on the back that illuminated in the dark.

Only a few of our childhood friends attended the party at the bowling alley bar. Many had moved away in their twenties and much further than a new neighborhood. Those who could afford went to college out of state hoping to experience life far from the nest. I went to a local community college, but when the opportunity arose, I flew on eager wings of escape to Richmond, Virginia, where I lived with old and new friends for one year. With little money and no viable prospects to remain, I returned home to Amityville, NY, and now I was escaping again on a new adventure. Hopefully this cross-country trek would take me away longer than one year.

CHAPTER II

At The Start

On the morning of June 9, 1979, John and I arrived at Amtrak in Penn Station with our packed panniers, boxed bicycles for storage and barely composed excitement we boarded the train bound for Richmond. Vague memories are recalled from that train ride other than it took approximately seven hours to reach our destination. As the train approached the stop in Richmond, recollection of John and I noticing houses near the track whiz by our window. At one of those houses we observed an elderly fellow in a wheelchair roll-up on his porch and blow into a bugle as our train passed by. We laughed watching the bearded invalid trump at the Amtrak as she coasted through. To this day, I wonder if he greeted each passing train in the same manner.

We disembarked from the train shortly after it arrived at the station, received our boxed bicycles and panniers from baggage, and quickly unpacked to begin the assembly process. Within a few minutes John and I assembled our bicycles, mounted the panniers, handlebar pouches and headed for my former residence on Three Chopt Road. I lived there in Richmond with another neighborhood friend from Amityville, Jerry, who John also knew from childhood. It took us less than one hour to pedal the hills from the Amtrak station to the west side of the city to Jerry's place on Three Chopt Road, so named as it split the city of Richmond in three places.

We pedaled slowly from the station partially due to the exhaustion from a long day of travel and because we got our first taste of steep climbs to cycle up. Eventually, we reached the house on Three Chopt Road as dusk settled in over the warm summer day. Jerry greeted us at the door, while John and I took the panniers off our bicycles and used our sleeping bags to crash in the living room. We rose early the next day and decided to pedal around town, get used to our wheels prior to attacking the TransAmerica trail.

Riding around the westside for a while, we stopped at a Seven Eleven for a breakfast snack. I suggested to John to pick-up two regular coffees and buttered rolls, while I stayed with our bicycles. Buttered rolls were common to order back home, but in the south such a request was silly, like asking someone to fetch a bucket of steam. I smiled as he walked into the store.

Standing watch over the bicycles, I chuckled when John returned with two coffees, no rolls, and a smirk of disgust on his face. We drank our coffees than mounted the bicycles and pedaled downtown to the Fan District of Richmond. We cycled by beautiful mansions, shops, and restaurants, avoiding cars and pedestrians. The roads were much steeper than what we were used to cycling on Long Island, so we strained slightly on the pedals and our pace was a bit slower on the unfamiliar terrain, staying in the lower gears of our ten speeds. We returned to the house on Three Chopt late in the afternoon, ate dinner with Jerry, our friend and host. We spent that night at the house using our sleeping bags planning to hit the trail in the morning.

Monday, June 11, 1979

John and I set out from Richmond at approximately 10:30 in the morning with our bicycles fully equipped, pedaling in the rain on Parham Road to US Route 1 while we were thoroughly soaked to the skin in the downpour. My Schwinn felt heavy, seventy-pounds heavy with fully packed panniers, (including clothes and sleeping bag), bicycle pump, full water bottle and handlebar pouch for personal items. We rested, taking five-minute breaks each hour so we could pedal an optimum mileage daily. We made our first stop at a General Store along US Route 1 to buy provisions, a little energy food for lunch. The rain ceased as we resumed our ride from the General Store, wearing the safety vests with the orange, reflective triangles that John acquired.

We pedaled on along Route 1 with coal trucks rumbling by us and I felt a woosh of air with each one roaring past. Eventually, one of the coal trucks ran me right off the shoulderless stretch of highway into a ditch and John pulled up alongside of me.

He dismounted his bike and asked with concern, "Are you alright?"

"Yeah, I'm okay," I responded, picking myself and my bicycle from the ground, "but I don't think I'm going to wear this vest anymore. I believe the damn truck drivers are using them for targets!"

"You're probably right." John acknowledged with a laugh and took his safety vest off too.

We stuffed the vests into our panniers and resumed the trek along the highway. At approximately 2:00 pm we reached Ashland, turning off Route 1 onto Route 657. While huffing and puffing up a gradual ascent in low gear, a kindly gentleman in a station wagon pulled up alongside and greeted us hello through his open car window. We stopped our bicycles and returned his greeting. The man recognized that we were biking the Bikecentennial trail and offered to put us up in his home located one-half mile from the direction we had come. As it was late in the day and still overcast from the earlier downpour, we gladly accepted the man's offer, following his station wagon back to his house.

We followed the station wagon into a driveway passing under a sign that read; VALHALLER'S and soon discovered that this was play on the kind man's name, Gene Haller. It turned out the Hallers were avid cycle touring enthusiasts having a touring bike custom made in France and shipped to their home in Ashland. Gene and his wife fed us a delicious dinner, provided us beds for the night and a bathroom for guests to wash up. After a breakfast of bacon and eggs, John and I thanked them for their hospitality, bid them farewell and departed VALHALLER'S at 9:00am.

Tuesday, June 12, 1979

It was beautifully sunny, yet not too hot a morning as we set out from the Haller's place and got back on the trail, pedaling through the small Virginia towns of Beaver Dam, Bumpass and into Louisa County beginning with the town of Buckner. As the day was so much nicer than our starting day, John and I forgot about our plan to rest five minutes on every hour, interrupting our hurried pace only for a lunch break. After lunch we pedaled into Mineral slowing down in the face of rolling hills and switchback roads to eventually reach Pendleton.

Checking the guidebook for Virginia, John realized we missed our campsite in Mineral priced at fifty cents per person. We decided to backtrack in hopes of finding the campsite but got misdirected by the street signs ending up in a small town called Christopher Run. As darkness set in, we made camp in that little town on the banks of Lake Anna for three dollars apiece.

It became abundantly clear that evening our training on the flat terrain of Long Island left us ill prepared to bicycle across country. I cannot speak for John, but I felt unequal to the challenge of the cycling I had done for the day, or what I was about to do through the Appalachian Mountains. I slept well that night having traveled forty to fifty miles from the Haller's place. Unfortunately, I pedaled through some of the steepest terrain thus far faced and felt some aching in my calves. Tomorrow, we hoped to reach Charlottesville, which was approximately forty-seven miles from Mineral.

Wednesday, June 13, 1979

We rose early to see the morning mist swarm over Lake Anna like a gossamer blanket rustled by a giant's restless sleep beneath. The coo of morning doves and the croak of frogs broke the silence, ringing in the new day with nature's chorus. I awoke, rose, ate a quick breakfast, and packed my sleeping bag onto my bicycle, drinking in the sights and sounds of the natural beauty around us. The refrain from an old church hymnal rang in my head in tempo with the croaking frogs and cooing doves.

"Rise and Shine and Give God Your Glory, Glory! Children of the Lord."

John and I broke camp and pedaled out of Christopher Run to Mineral and back into Pendleton returning to our five-to-one rest ratio for the third day of our adventure. The TransAmerica bike trail referred to this section as predominantly rollercoaster hills and they did not exaggerate. We encountered hills that defiantly loomed before us and I swore hearing them laugh at our feeble attempt to climb over their tops. We pedaled some fifty miles through the Piedmont/Coastal Plain section and happily stopped for lunch at a cafe' in Palmyra around 2:00pm.

Studying the map in the café' we realized it was another thirty miles to reach Charlottesville. We quickly gobbled the food orders and returned to our bicycles deciding to take no more five-to-one rest stops for the remainder of the day. The continuing route into Charlottesville took us through more winding hills with steep climbs and my legs felt like jelly, as I pulled-up and pushed-down upon the pedals, again and again.

We saw two other bikers heading in the opposite direction, pedaling east, and waved to them as we passed each other. I thought they probably would not find many places to stop past Palmyra, since there were few services between Mineral and us. Even though the road into Charlottesville was narrow, shoulderless and switchback the cars seem to give the road conditions, or we cyclist little consideration. They blew past our bikes at too high a speed and would lag us, only when traffic would not accommodate their right-of-way. In those brief moments, I felt empowered over the gas guzzling automobiles.

John and I bicycled through Charlottesville for another five to ten miles to a campground called Lake Reynovia. After setting up camp I forced my aching body to climb on my bicycle and pedal down to the campground entrance, the general store, and a public telephone. I placed a collect call to Patti, checking on her condition and gave her my love. Upon concluding the call, I hung-up the telephone receiver, exited the phone booth and shuffled into the general store where I purchased hotdogs, baked beans and a sixpack of beer. After John and I ate the franks and beans for dinner and split the sixpack, I immediately crashed, as the beer proved to be a very effective sedative leaving me to fall out unconscious, passing quickly beyond the aching pains of my fatigued body. I am sure I dreamt of Patti while falling asleep and in my thoughts of her, I began to understand how much I truly loved the pregnant girl in Amityville.

Thursday, June 14, 1979

We stayed in camp today resting up after the strenuous ride from Lake Anna to Charlottesville. John studied the map and estimated that we traveled over eighty miles yesterday. My body still ached a little, but not nearly as much as it did last night before I fell unconscious. That sleep certainly helped, still neither of us wanted another full day of cycling, so we opted to pedal down to Monticello and visit the architectural masterpiece of Thomas Jefferson.

Upon arrival at Monticello, we took a tour of the property and house. We were led in a tour group into the main hall of the house. A great clock designed by Jefferson was mounted above the entrance with a large gong set on the rooftop, which (it was said) could be heard chiming three miles away. The weights for this large, pendulum clock was canon shot hung by chain and the hall floor had two holes at each corner for the canon shot to pass through to complete the time cycle. In Jefferson's day the hall served as a reception area for visitors also containing a museum of sorts with artifacts of American natural history, western civilization, and Native American cultures. In addition to being President and Statesman for America and a founding father, Jefferson was also an architect and archaeologist.

Jefferson ordered the floor in the main hall be painted a green grass color and the room contains a balcony connecting two mezzanine-level wings with the ceiling featuring an eagle and stars pattern. Next on the tour was the South Square Room also known as Martha Jefferson Randolph's Sitting Room. This room featured various colonial furnishings including Martha's sewing table, and her portrait hung above the fireplace, The walls of the sitting room were painted in a soft, blue pastel, which brightened my mood as I stepped inside.

Our tour group was next led into the library, part of Jefferson's suite of private rooms consisting of the Book Room, the Greenhouse, the Cabinet, and his Bedroom. The suite's plan was based on an octagon pattern, a favorite in architecture for Jefferson. The library, or Book Room housed some 6,000 books collected by Jefferson, as he was an avid reader. Next to the Library was the South Piazza, or Greenhouse, which was flanked by two Venetian porches.

The fifth room on the tour was the Cabinet, or Jefferson's office used for reading, writing, architectural drafting, and scientific observation. The room contained a reading and writing arrangement that included a revolving chair, table with revolving top, a revolving bookstand made in Monticello joinery, and a mechanical copying device which he invented. The room also held a vast collection of scientific instruments including a microscope and telescope.

Jefferson's bed was built into an alcove, as were all the beds throughout the house since he saw beds as a waste of room space. However, only his alcove bed separated two rooms, roll out one side and he was in his Cabinet, roll out the other into his bedroom. The bedroom furnishings consisted of the alcove bed, clotheshorse in closet, obelisk clock at the foot of the bed enabling Jefferson to get out of bed with the sun, crimson silk counterpane with fringe (designed by Jefferson) covered the bed, and mirrors used to maximize the natural light.

The seventh room on the tour was the Parlor used for celebrative gatherings in the Jefferson household. The room featured a special parquet floor of beech and cherry wood and the single-acting double door. When one door is opened, or closed, the other follows in a mirror like fashion. Both the parquet floor and double-doors were designed by Thomas Jefferson and were beautifully featured in the Parlor. The last three rooms presented on the tour were the Dining Room, the Tea Room, and the North Octagonal Room. Most of the rooms on the first floor of the three-story mansion that served the dual purpose of ventilation, or doorways when opened.

After the tour of Monticello and the grounds, John and I picked up our dirty clothes at camp and bicycled into Charlottesville. We located a laundromat downtown and split the fee to wash and dry our clothes, careful to separate whites and color in the washing machines. After doing our laundry we stopped at the town Post Office to pickup the first prearranged shipment of food. John collected the self-addressed package and we started back to camp, stopping again at a health food store to purchase dry fruit and nut mixtures. After our purchases we headed back to the camp at Lake Reynovia by way of Constitute Run. We rested for a short while upon returning to the camp and then repacked the panniers onto our bicycles. I telephoned Patti prior to dinner, which made me feel good, almost ache free when I heard her voice once more. Tomorrow, we hope to make up some miles in compensation for our free day from the trail.

Friday, June 15, 1979

We broke camp at approximately 9:00am biking to Charlottesville for breakfast and departed there by 10:00 in the morning. We rode steady today covering roughly sixty miles of very hilly terrain and just past midday we encountered the steepest climbs thus far on the trip. At approximately 2:30pm we reached Afton, which I forever refer to as the town of many pains.

This is a small niche community surrounded by steep climbs in the heart of the southern Appalachians. Neither John nor I could manage pedaling up the steep inclines of Afton, so we walked our bikes for three miles with dry mouths, throbbing legs and dripping wet bodies. At this time, I doubted my conviction to complete this bicycle adventure; yet, I persevered, pushing my bicycle along the upgrade.

We met an elderly man at the end of our climb who directed us a little further up the rise, a house John recalled from the guidebook, the home of June "Cookie Lady" Curry. The Cookie Lady lives in a house on the Bikecentennial route, near the top of Afton Mountain and she offers hospitality to cyclists by way of a cool drink, and lots of fresh baked cookies. We sat in her parlor and drank her offerings of fruit punch and lemonade in small disposable cups, we drank, and drank, and drank some more, attempting to quench our unquenchable thirst.

John and I ate her cookies as well and I recall that they were delicious, freshly baked oatmeal cookies that seem to melt in my mouth. She also served us sandwiches at no charge, so we had our lunch for free. June took our picture with an instamatic camera and mounted on the wall of her parlor along with hundreds of others she snapped-off since 1976. I remember seeing some unusual photos on her parlor wall of all the adventurers who stopped by during their trek. There was one fellow traveling the TransAmerica trail riding a mule and another guy doing the trip on a unicycle, I imagined that guy's butt hurt bad, riding the single-wheel cycle across country. I wondered whose butt was sorer, the fellow on the mule, the guy with the unicycle, or mine? Although I purchased a Brookes leather saddle for my Schwinn, which contoured to my butt, I still got sore after a week of pedaling through the Appalachians.

I heard the Cookie Lady on Afton Mountain was still offering hospitality to passing cyclists in the early 2000s. I suspect she accrued a veritable museum of cyclists' imagery over those many years. Sadly, June passed away in 2012 and TransAmerica adventurers today shall not experience the generosity of that selfless, compassionate lady- the Angel of the TransAmerica Trail. John and I coasted down from the top of Afton Mountain preparing for more step climbs ahead.

We continued on Route 750 along a few more switchback turns and rises to the Blue Ridge Parkway and Shenandoah Skyline. Soon I was feeling the aches and pains of mountain biking again, as we ascended 1000 ... 2000 ... 3000 feet, using each downhill run to the fullest advantage to surmount the next rise. Panoramic views of the Blue Ridge were breathtaking, which made the strain in cycling worth every aching stroke of the pedals. We eventually made camp at Meadow Mountain, and I slept very well that night. Admittedly, I felt like tossing my bicycle in the woods and catching the bus back to New York, but somehow, I persevered.

Saturday, June 16, 1979

Around 9:30am we got started again, riding through the last leg of the George Washington Forest, still climbing and coasting, climbing, and coasting through the moderate grades of the Blue Ridge Parkway. At one point I playfully pedaled hard past John and accidently bumped his bike causing his pannier rack to bend into his rear tire. My foolish act resulted in two of his spokes to break and a forty-five-minute delay for John to make repairs. I believe that John wanted to throw my bike in the woods at that point, so I humbly apologized and begged his forgiveness.

We got started again after John replaced the spokes on his rear wheel and we finally reached the point where we exited the Blue Ridge Parkway. It was around midday when we made an incredible downhill run on a thirteen percent grade that carried us approximately three miles in an exhilarating descent. The ride was nerve-racking and at the same time incredibly fun where I could only guess at our speed as we rode on our breaks preventing a total loss of control. The steep descent ended in the town of Vesuvius, but in a way, I hoped it would go on and on. I realize in reflection that some people desire a continuance of stimulation that frightens and excites. Such people never get tired of riding on rollercoasters or other types of thrill-rides, I guess I am, or was one of those types of people as that is the way I felt about the downhill run to Vesuvius.

In Vesuvius we rested a short while then proceeded into Cross-Marl Creek to the Steels Tavern Truck Stop for lunch. After we bicycled another twenty-two miles of climbs and downhills to Lexington, Virginia. The campsite in Lexington was missed, so John suggested staying the night in a motel. Since it was getting dark, I agreed despite my meager holdings.

Sunday, June 17, 1979

We checked out of the Motel at 9:00am and cycled to Natural Bridge, Virginia approximately fifteen miles from Lexington and took a few hours to tour this wonder of nature. An awe-inspiring sight considered to be one million years old, a mammoth edifice fashioned by Mother Nature over countless years. The great arch consists of thirty-six thousand tons of limestone with a height rising to an impressive two hundred and fifteen feet. The bridge is ninety feet long and runs from fifty to one hundred and fifty feet wide. It is impossible for me to express words describing the beauty and splendor of this natural monument, it must be seen to be truly enjoyed.

After our tour of Natural Bridge, we bicycled another thirteen miles to Buchanan. Enroute to that destination we encountered a good old boy in a Chevy pickup, who drove alongside, mumbling inaudibly toward us from his open window. This stalker in the Chevy gave me an eerie feeling and I kept remembering the sequence of the final scenes from the film Easy Rider. John and I were quite happy when our pursuing heckler turned and drove off from our route. In Buchanan, we could not locate the suggested campsite in the guidebook, rather than spending on another Motel room, we camped in a field alongside the James River. It began to rain slightly as we set up our camp, so sleeping did not come easy. We pedaled about twenty-eight miles today and slept lightly due to the damp conditions.

Monday, June 18, 1979

John and I got an early start in the steady drizzle falling since the night before. Determined to turn some miles, we decided to resume our five to one rest ratio. The two of us poured it on through the last leg of the Shenandoah Valley into the Blue Ridge Highlands pedaling mostly uphill. The rain finally stopped by midday yet remained hazy and muggy.

We made camp at Radford City Park clocking about seventy miles for the day. Appearing as it may rain again, we are sleeping under a shelter in the park on picnic tables.

CHAPTER III
Leaving Virginia

Tuesday, June 19, 1979

Today is my birthday and I am all of twenty-four years old. We agreed not to travel any distance today in honor of the occasion and cycled a mere twelve miles to a campsite called Meadow Creek after picking up supplies at the Radford General Store. It began to rain again after we set up camp. John purchased some beer, a gift for my birthday, and I plan getting good and drunk, as there isn't much to do camping in the rain. God, I miss Patti.

Wednesday, June 20, 1979

We hoped to make Wytheville quicker than normal by leaving the trail and opting for the highway. We broke camp pedaling back into Radford to do laundry around 10:30am and ate lunch afterward. We departed Radford at 1:00pm by way of Highway 11. John and I made really good time pedaling through Dublin, Virginia into Pulaski in an hour flat then took our five-minute break and resumed the trek on 11 out of Pulaski into Draper by way of Draper Mountain.

Eventually, Highway 11 merged into Interstate 81, so we were forced to find an alternate road to travel. After studying the map John found Route 100 as an alternative to the Interstate. Unfortunately, this took us southeast of Wytheville and we ended up in Sylvatus thirty miles from our destination. We made camp at a R-J Campsite, totally disgusted with wasting a day of cycling by attempting a shortcut via the highway.

Thursday, June 21, 1979

We started out at 9:00am in a heavy downpour. Despite the rain we pedaled hard to get back on track bicycling on Route 607 to Highway 52. Our route bypassed Interstate 81 in the right direction and from there we took Route 610. We followed that road right into Wytheville and made camp at High Bridge, one mile south of town. By 1:00pm we were in the village and decided not to go any further in the rain.

Friday, June 22, 1979

John and I broke camp taking the short jaunt into Wytheville to the Post Office. We mailed some things home to lighten the panniers. I sent home most of my clothes, anything that was unessential for the trip including my cycling helmet. A few articles of clothing were retained, to have a change of clothes on my adventure. I even discarded my bicycle kickstand, which was more psychological than a significant weight reduction. John also discarded items from his panniers and mailed back his helmet as well then picked up another food parcel that he mailed to himself.

We met another westbound cyclist at the Post Office a fellow named Craig from New Jersey who was doing the trek solo. Craig decided to join us on our journey, and we became a trio heading to Marion on Route 11. John heard there was a Bluegrass Festival in Marion at the Post Office, so we started pedaling around 11:00am. The three of us arrived in Marion after three to four hours of heavy riding only to find there was no scheduled Bluegrass Festival that day. The misinformation regarding the festival disappointed, but did not deter us, as Craig new of a church hostel in Damascus and with a little luck we could make it there before dark.

At 2:30pm we departed Marion hoping to cover twenty-five to thirty miles before nightfall. We continued on 11 until we reached Glade Spring then exited onto Route 91 only twelve miles from Damascus. It was overcast all day and we pedaled a good pace along 91. Suddenly, the road transformed from smooth pavement to rough stone forcing us to dismount and walk our bicycles. Just at that moment the gray skies opened and let loose more rain. It began as a light drizzle, but a rumble of thunder forewarned of a heavy downpour. Eventually the smooth pavement returned, so we mounted our bikes as the sky darkened and the rumbling thunder increased in frequency. The drizzle eventually expanded into a pouring rain as we arrived in Damascus and searched for the church hostel. Following Craig's lead, we found the hostel before being fully drenched in the rain.

Saturday, June 23, 1979

We decided to stay at the hostel and get cleaned up and rearrange the supplies in our panniers. They had a shower at the hostel with hot water too, so the three of us were able to get squeaky clean. Fortunately, the hostel was mostly vacant at that time. After showering, changing my clothes and repacking my panniers, I realized my funds dwindled to a low amount, so I decided to buy only what I needed. It became quite clear to me that the $700.00 I brought initially was not nearly enough. The hostel began to fill up in the afternoon with hikers from the Appalachian Trail. Fortunately, having already used the shower we did not have to compete with the other hostel guests in getting cleaned up.

We conversed with some of the hikers at the hostel. A fellow named Rick was from Birmingham, Alabama and was quitting the trail at this point to hitchhike to the beach. Rick was good natured with the appearance of a true mountain man that seemed to me a bit out of place for a beach destination with shoulder length hair and long scraggily beard. He was in the company of another hiker from Huntington, Long Island who was also quitting the trail to go to the beach.

The two hikers referred to themselves as Trail Monsters since they overpacked (at least 50 lbs.) with luxuries, clothes, and junk food to backpack the Appalachian Trail. Rick referred to the hikers in contrast to himself and his buddy as Trail Rats, those who packed light to hike swiftly and efficiently on the trail. One such hiker was at the hostel; his name was Lee and he was all of sixteen years old. Lee was gutsy, who was hiking the Appalachians from Georgia to Pennsylvania and going it alone. The prior summer he hiked the northern half starting in Maine and this year he was completing the trek. Lee was a serious, outdoorsy teenager and an experienced hiker, he steadfastly walked as much as twenty miles a day even if it meant hiking in night's darkness.

Sunday, June 24, 1979

I awoke around 9:00 in the morning to eat breakfast with John and Craig. It was still gray and rainy outside and it seemed to me that it rained more often than not during our passage through Virginia. We decided we were going to leave the hostel and Damascus by noontime while Craig attended services that morning at the Baptist Church associated with the hostel, but John and I declined to join him. Eight more hikers arrived at the hostel from the trail while Lee and the two Trail Monsters departed the hostel when we did. The hostel in Damascus proved to be one of the best rests stops thus far on the bicycle trip where one could relax and commune in conversation with new acquaintances.

It was still raining when we got back on the road pedaling onto Route 91 with thoughts of making camp in the Jefferson National Forest Preserve that night. A portion of 91 was under construction, covered with gravel and mud. While pedaling through this section of bad road I slipped and fell hard in the muddy gravel. As the road became impassible the three of us dragged our bikes through the gravelly muck for two miles, praying that the rain would stop, Eventually, we reached rideable road, mounted our bikes, and pedaled on.

From 91 we hit Route 803 while the rain intensified falling relentlessly upon our trio pressing ever forward. We reached Route 80 in a town called Hayters with the rain continuing, incessantly pelting us like darts of moisture stinging our flesh. We decided to make camp anywhere we could to avoid the deluge, so Craig volunteered to knock on doors and beg for shelter. No one answered at the first house he called on, so he tried the next, a country church, Ironically, the church refused us shelter suggesting we go to a campsite some miles down the road.

Craig noticed a Sheriff's car in the drive of a house across the street from the church and opted to give them a try. He knocked on the front door and a halfdressed man answered. Craig asked if we could pitch a tent in his yard, or if he could provide shelter from the rain. The Sheriff saw the three of us standing in the showers like soaked stray cats and offered us respite in an abandoned house at the back of his property. We gladly accepted and thankfully shall sleep indoors, comfortably, and dry tonight. We travelled about twenty-five miles today and still have approximately sixty miles to reach the Kentucky border.

Monday, June 25, 1979

We awoke early gathered our belongings, ate a breakfast of cold cereal, and departed the abandoned house by 9:00am. Thank God it had stopped raining and the sun peaked shyly from behind the clouds. We stopped at a country store at the base of Clinch Mountain for some juice prior to making the climb up on our bicycles. A man pulled up to the store in a pickup truck while we drank our juice and John asked him what the road was like going up the mountain.

"Well young feller," spouted the man, "dat road yonder is hard … five miles of curve like a snake's back. You-a-ridin' dem by-cycles up dar?"

John nodded and the man continued with a smile, "Well, I wish you-awl da-besta-luck."

The man entered the store as we finished our drinks mounted our bicycles and started up the mountain. The man met at the store was not kidding the road immediately began to wind as it rose up the mountain. The three of us paced ourselves to make the climb and I shifted to second gear in order to crawl the steep incline. For the entire ride up the mountain coal trucks jockeyed by us in both directions making the difficult climb even more hazardous. Finally, after what seemed and endless, serpentine crawl up the Clinch we reached the summit and began an exhilarating four and one-half mile downhill run.

The road like the uphill side continued curving like a snake, steeply on the descent like the best of thrill rides, but with a new condition. Wet spots crept onto the pavement of the road leaching from the rock walls bordering it adding yet another hazard. Coming around a sharp turn on the downhill passage I almost dropped my bicycle as it slid across a wet patch. At the same time an oncoming coal truck almost rolled over me and the outcome was way too close for comfort. I managed to pull the bicycle backup beneath me as the truckdriver stood heavy on his breaks and I just avoided being flattened like a pancake. After regaining my balance on the bike, I proceeded in completing the downhill run-on Clinch Mountain.

A little way past the mountain we stopped at a Methodist Church in the town of Elk Garden. The Minister of the church gave us fresh water and recounted how he helped cyclists running the trail for the last couple of years. Although the Minister was not as prominently known as the Cookie Lady to those traveling the Bikecentennial Trail, his offer of fresh water was more than welcome in the muggy summer heat. He also informed us of the terrain ahead and another mountain just past the town of Honaker called the Big A.

"My Daddy lives beyond the Big A," announced the Minister, "his house is right across from the general store."

We thanked the Minister for the refreshing water and the information regarding his Daddy and set out again along Route 80. We stopped in Honaker for lunch then pressed on over the Big A. The climb was not as difficult as the Clinch Mountain and we were soon down on the other side. We stopped at the general store and met the Minister's father who lived across the street. A spry old man of eighty-two who boasted of riding a motorcycle just two years earlier on the Big A. We spoke with the old man for awhile and discovered that we faced another three miles uphill before it dropped off again.

My heart sank when I heard the news regarding the road ahead of us as I felt sick from pedaling uphill. Admittedly I became stronger bicycling through the Appalachians and had not thought about quitting and throwing my bike in the woods since I faced the Blue Ridge. However, the mere thought of crawling up steep, switchback paths carved into mountains with my bicycle set in low gear caused my body to shake with anticipation of the pain it would bring.

Taking to the trail again we started the climb up the hills from the general store. Another cyclist came up strong from behind us and introduced himself as Larry from Rockford, Illinois. Larry was a bit older than us I guessed that he was in his thirties, and he gave himself two months to bicycle the entire trail. Larry said that he tried to make between seventy and one hundred miles a day on his Trek bicycle and I believed that he might very well achieve his goal.

The four of us pedaled hard up US 80 toward the Breaks Interstate Park with Larry leading the way, setting a feverish pace for our group.

We were moving at a real good clip and soon found ourselves a mere fifteen miles from the Breaks. The last eight miles felt like they were all uphill and once again I was reduced to a crawl with my Schwinn set to the lowest gear. The aches found their usual place on the muscles and joints of my legs and once again they throbbed with pain. We eventually reached the Park at 8:30pm to setup camp in the dark. John, Craig, and I traveled around fifty miles for the day while Larry claimed he had clocked eighty-five. We camped alongside two other cyclists who were camped in the Breaks since the previous night, The two cyclists were leaving in the morning and were planning a one-hundred-mile day, so Larry asked to team-up with them and depart our company. Larry seemed like a nice guy, very energetic and very much in a hurry, too much of a hurry for us so we accepted his choice to ride on with the others. We all talked about the trip ahead eventually falling asleep from exhaustion. Tomorrow we would enter a new state leaving the steep and winding roads behind us.

As I lay half asleep in my bag, I reflected on the sites I saw and people I encountered as I pedaled through the State of Virginia. I remembered the marvel of Natural Bridge, the impressiveness of Jefferson's Monticello, and the beauty and pain of cycling the Blue Ridge Parkway and the Shenandoah Skyline. I thought about some of the people I met along the way, those who were incredibly friendly to total strangers. People like the Hallers of Ashland, the Cookie Lady of Afton, the Trail Monsters at the hostel in Damascus and the Minister of the Methodist Church in Elk Garden. As I fell asleep, I wondered if the trail ahead would be as memorable as the one, I left behind? I hoped so.

CHAPTER IV
Passage Through the Bluegrass State

Tuesday, June 26, 1979

Craig, John, and I departed the Breaks about 8:00 in the morning. Larry had lit out earlier with the two cyclists, so we were unable to bid him farewell. Our trio cycled on mostly a downhill grade into Elkhorn City, Kentucky where we stopped for breakfast. The breakfast consisted of good old homestyle cooking, hominy grits, biscuits and gravy, scrambled eggs with ham. I challenge anyone traveling through the south not to encounter a homestyle breakfast that includes grits with biscuits and gravy. These dishes are common fare in the Southland, yet I did not find them impressive to my palate.

Biscuits and gravy are a popular breakfast dish in the south. The dish consists of soft dough biscuits covered in white gravy, made from the drippings of cooked pork. Then the grits. What are grits? A question I asked myself sitting in that southern comfort establishment at Elkhorn City. Many years later I discovered where grits come from as you likely could not tell after tasting the granular food. Alone grits are pretty tasteless boiled in water and fried in lard, so eating them gives little hint to their origin. Grits are drawn from corn kernels. When corn is soaked in lye and the casing has been removed it becomes hominy. The lye is rinsed thoroughly from the corn and the kernels are left to harden. While hardening the hominy swells then it is ground up to the texture of tiny pellets, or granules. These tiny granules are boiled in water, milk, and butter to become hominy grits. Grits are a staple of the Southland, however raised in a suburb of New York, I prefer a freshly baked bagel.

After our homestyle breakfast we slowly mounted our bicycles and pedaled out of Elkhorn City on Russell Street toward Route 197. Along this route we encountered more rolling hills, brutally hot sun, and several barking dogs that attacked our bicycles as we feverishly pedaled by them. Our first encounter with dogs on the trail attacking more than once today from the many farms we passed. It made cycling difficult with farm dogs nipping at your ankles. It was at this time I realized I needed some defense from future canine attacks.

Later, along the route we hit a three-mile climb on very poorly paved road. After a short stretch of very difficult pedaling our group decided to walk our bicycles, which was a wise move as the last mile uphill featured no pavement at all. The downhill on that section of 197 also was a barren stretch without pavement for a mile, or two. We walked our bicycles in descent until the pavement reappeared then we coasted on our bikes into Verge, Kentucky and made camp in a churchyard around 6:30 that evening. Craig, John, and I bicycled approximately forty miles today.

Wednesday, June 27, 1979

Planning another easy day, we targeted an AYH (American Youth Hostel) in Pippa Passes, which was approximately thirty miles from our location. We broke camp at 8:00am and started out in a westerly direction confronted by three, bad uphill climbs through the depressed area of eastern Kentucky. The first uphill hit us early after Hellier in a town called Lookout, we hit the second mountain rise in Bevinsville and the third in Pippa Passes and the one at Pippa was the hardest to cycle up.

Fortunately, there was a package store called Last Chance – Carry Out at the top of a mountain at the line of a dry county. Last Chance sold cold beer and alcohol, and I'm sure was a popular stop for most cyclists traveling the TransAmerica Trail. We certainly stopped to drink a cold beer before pressing on.

We reached our destination at 1:00pm and visited a junior college close to the AYH called Alice Lloyd College. The school was quaint, but beautiful in the rustic setting of Appalachia. A graduate named Keith

Bradley Banks gave us a tour of the campus and invited us to attend the play his theater group was performing that afternoon on the campus grounds. Keith explained that the play was a short piece, a traditional Appalachian play known as Jack-Tales, and we agreed to watch the performance.

The play was performed on an outdoor stage and was entitled, Jack and the Three Sillies. There were five actors including Keith performing a total of twentyfive speaking parts in this one-half hour performance. The pace of the play was very quick and brimming with Appalachian dialect prominently found in the JackTales. Phrases like "I reckon, outdoin', yonder, down the road apiece," and "actin' unruly" appeared throughout the dialogue of the short play, and I "figgered" to understand most of the mountain speech.

The plot was simple. Jack, the main character (played by Keith) is about to marry a wealthy farmer's daughter named Buttons. When he finds Buttons and her parents extremely silly, he vows to leave and not return unless he finds three sillies, "more silly than you three sillies!" He travels the country and meets an old woman trying to capture sunlight in boxes to brighten the inside of her windowless house. He moves on to find a family of milkmaids who have trouble counting to five and newlyweds with feuding in-laws. He meets a man who spends hours a day trying to put on his pants and numerous silly people who make Buttons, and her parents seem almost intelligent. The play was a humorous delight and well done by the Appalachian Theater Group. Craig, John, and I returned to the AYH after the performance to find a lot of noisy youths staying there making our chances of peaceful sleep slim at best.

Thursday, June 28, 1979

We found an Army-Navy Surplus store in Pippa Passes where we bought some items to thwart the dogs attacking us along the trail. John and Craig bought some pepper spray, and I found a mini bullwhip, also called a snakewhip for $20.00. Although this purchase put a big dent into my meager funds, I deemed it a necessity to stave off the attacking farmdogs. It was ideal for use aboard my tenspeed bicycle, a braided whip at three feet of length and separated into four fly leads at the cracker end.

My snakewhip was just the right size to crack at dogs without getting caught in the bike's tires or gears or hurting my attackers.

We departed Pippa Passes around 9:00am and biked down to Route 80 toward Hindman. For a photo op we stopped on 80 at a town sign which read: Dwarf. Craig donned his rain poncho, sat on his knees beneath the sign and placed a pair of sneakers protruding out from the poncho's bottom edge where his feet would be. He had John take his picture with his 35mm camera depicting a little person standing before the "Dwarf" sign. After our creative photo break, we proceeded enroute reaching Hazard by 2:30pm where we stopped for lunch at a Pizza Hut. We devoured the slices we ordered as a man entered the eatery and greeted us with a smile.

"Hey there young fellers," he asked, "are you by-cycling cross country?"

We nodded affirmatively and he continued, "Well I just passed three other fellers back a piece in my pickup. Oh, I guess bout fifteen miles back yonder and them dang fools was tryin' to hitchhike with their by-cycles in tow. You don't know those three fellers, do ya?"

We shook our heads no, finished our lunch, departed the Pizza Hut mounted our bicycles and pressed onto Buckhorn State Park rather than waiting to meet the three cyclists behind us. Some farm dogs attacked us three times on the first half of today's cycling, and I got a chance to use my snakewhip. It worked better than I imagined, better than the pepper spray that Craig and John bought. Just a flick of my wrist with the whip crack near Spot's or Rover's nose and they ran full speed in the opposite direction. I even had fun using my snakewhip from the seat of my ten-speed, made me feel like a drover in the outback herding critters.

The feeling became more apparent when one of the attacking farm animals turned out to be a Billie goat. I pedaled at the ready with the whip on my bicycle hearing the dog barking increase with intensity behind me. Yet, my preparedness was quickly altered when I heard the jingling of a bell among the barks of dogs. I turned to see a determined goat on the heels of the dog pack with his head lowered displaying his horns in a menacing manner. The sight caused me to laugh so hard that I had difficulty pedaling to stay ahead of my attackers, suddenly the whip seemed like overkill.

After lunch I began to feel ill enroute to Buckhorn, so my co-cyclists agreed for my sake to stop at the next available campsite instead of going on to the State Park. Unfortunately, the next available camp was about seven miles of bad road followed by a two-mile unpaved downhill run. John led us to the campsite, a nice area on a lake that was free of charge. We setup camp with the tent John and I took turns carrying and made a cook-fire for our dinner of rice and navy beans.

As we began to eat our dinner a Park Ranger pulled up into the campsite exited his vehicle and walked over to chat with us. The Ranger was young, did not look much older than us and appeared very enthusiastic regarding the TransAmerica Bicycle Trail. He stayed and talked to us while we ate our dinner until a pickup truck pulled up alongside his cruiser. Three cyclists unloaded from the back of the pickup as the Park Ranger drove off exiting the camping area and the truck followed behind him. The three cyclists we heard about at the Pizza Hut caught up to us.

The three were from Kentucky and began their cycling trip at Virginia Beach, VA. The leader of their group introduced himself as Bobby who seemed a little older than the others and sported a bushy moustache with curly brown hair. Bobby claimed to be a graduate from Eastern University out of Richmond, Kentucky and his partners Scott and Jim as semi-professional students from the same school.

"We're kind a partying across the country," admitted Scott, "just tryin' to see how fer we get till we run outa beer money."

Scott was a real friendly fellow even more so than his co-cyclists and he invited us to join them for a party that evening, their treat. We happily agreed so Jim and Bobby hitched back to town for a beer run while Scott stayed back in the camp with us. As we waited and talked Scott reached into his pack withdrawing a candy bar, a "Zero" bar and offered one each to our trio. We politely declined, free beer was more than enough, and we thought not to impose on his hospitality further by taking his candy too.

Scott removed the candy wrapper revealing a chocolate candy bar with a frosty white coating. He bit into it slowly as an expression of ecstasy lit up his face.

"Mmmmmmm Zero," Scott exclaimed, "gives you a whole new outlook on life."

"You sound like a commercial," I remarked, "you must be a stockholder."

"No, these are really great!" He asserted after another bite, "You sure you don't want one?"

I agreed to take him up on his second offer and Scott hurriedly tore the wrapper away handing me one of his Zero bars. As I bit into the white frosted chocolate Scott grinned at me and nodded.

"Taste great, doesn't it?" Scott commented, "It does give you a new outlook, huh?"

I nodded in agreement as I ate the Zero bar and Scott helped himself to another. Eventually Bobby and Jim returned with two cases of beer and some food for their dinner. We proceeded to drink and drink, drinking up all the beer between the six of us while Bobbi, Jim and Scott ate the food brought back with the beer for their dinner. Eventually, I fell asleep no longer feeling sick. I am not sure if it was the Zero bar, or all the beer I consumed, but my illness dissipated that evening.

Friday, June 29, 1979

We awoke with beer hangovers by midday and slowly broke camp moving lethargically like desert tortoises in the heat of an unforgiving sun. Hangovers are not conducive to bicycle touring and beer hangovers are probably worse with combined ailments of throbbing head and body bloat from mass consumption. The six of us packed up our camp and crawled out of the park dragging our bicycles up the three miles of gravel and dirt road to where we finally reached pavement. We agreed to bicycle into Hyden, Kentucky and rest up with a late lunch. Hoping after a restaurant meal our hangovers would subside and we could get some serious mileage in before day's end.

It seems that Bobby, Scott, and Jim did a lot of bicycles hitchhiking to come as far as they did for as soon as we reached the pavement they fanned out on the road and began thumbing for a ride. Bobby and Jim pedaled approximately one-quarter mile ahead of us and walked their bikes while our trio hung back with Scott to beg for a ride into Hyden. After awhile Scott flagged down a Ford Pickup and the driver agreed to take the four of us onboard with our bicycles. We climbed onto the back of the pickup with our bikes and the truck drove us into Hyden. We waved at Bobby and Jim as the Ford passed them on the road.

John, Craig, and I felt a bit guilty riding in the back of a truck with perfectly good bicycles when Scott seemed perfectly at home with this mode of transportation on the TransAmerica Trail. However, it was only a ten-mile ride into town, so our egos were not terribly bruised from our one time only bicycle hitchhiking experience. The pickup dropped us off in front of a fast-food joint where we put up our bicycles and walked inside for a quick lunch.

Within fifteen minutes Bobby and Jim joined us for lunch in the eatery having bummed a ride from a second pickup truck. After eating we headed outside to plan how much further we would cycle prior to nightfall, but before we could decide it began to rain. It poured down the rest of the day, we got stuck in Hyden, opting to take shelter in a nearby pool hall/café. In the shelter from the storm, we met a local girl named Rhonda who offered us accommodation in an abandoned house behind her sister's trailer. John, Craig, and I accepted her offer while Scott and the others found an apartment to stay the night instead. We drank more beer (hair of the dog) before parting company.

In Hyden we met an attractive girl with blonde hair staying in a house near to the place that Rhonda lent us. She was sitting on the front porch swing as we pedaled by and her beauty immediately captured our attention. She had an angelic face and when she smiled her allure seem to intensify with an irradiant glow. After we set up in our abandoned house Craig and I headed back down to where the pretty girl was sitting and introduced ourselves.

Her name was Jill. She was from Ohio and staying a few weeks in town with relatives. Jill was even prettier close up with silky blonde hair and striking blue eyes that sparkled when she smiled or laughed. Our conversation lasted a few hours and helped ease my loneliness from the great distance between me and Patti. Leaving gorgeous Jill on the porch that evening, I promised myself I would call Patti in the morning.

Saturday, June 30, 1979

We met up with Bobby, Scott, and Jim in town around 8:30 in the morning ate breakfast and hung around until 10:00am. I used a pay phone and called Patti collect in Amityville. It was great hearing her voice again and I wished so much to hold her in my arms, to feel the warmth of her body and the soft touch of her smooth skin against mine. We chatted for a little while until I felt the loneliness swell up in me like a sad, queasy reflex, so I said goodbye to Patti before the melancholy overwhelmed me.

John, Craig, and I planned to make for Berea, Kentucky to complete one third of our passage through the state. The other three were undecided how far they wanted to travel but wanted to reach their hometown of Richmond by nightfall. Our group of six bicycled on the Parkway toward Manchester and reached the town at approximately 1:00pm. Just before we reached the town Jim busted two spokes on his rear wheel, so we spent around three hours in town to have lunch and repair Jim's bike. John trued his wheel since he was better at the task than anyone else and certainly more skilled than Jim at straightening the tire rim. We departed Manchester at 4:00pm and were within thirty-five miles of Berea by 7:00 that evening.

At this point, Bobby, Scott, and Jim had enough bicycling for the day, dismounted from their bikes and began hitching along Route 421. We parted company with them and cycled on reaching Berea by 9:30 that night having ridden seventy miles that day. As we pedaled toward our campsite, one and one-half miles west of town, we met two bikers cycling east on the trail. They were seasoned cyclists from San Francisco with powerful legs including magnificently muscular calves. The two claimed to travel one hundred miles a day, or more and each carried around seventy-five pounds of gear on their bicycles.

They used State maps to navigate instead of the guides provided by the TransAmerica Trail and had covered most of the cross-country distance in a mere five and one-half weeks. I could only dream about being that efficient on a long-distance bicycle trip. Still, it left me to wonder if they were burning up the miles that quickly were they truly enjoying the experience of bicycling across country? It seemed to me that the primary motivation for their type of cycling was daily distance and endurance, and not appreciation of the countryside, or the people encountered along the way. That night I reflected on those two eastbound cyclists and their fast-paced approach to the bicycle adventure, and I did not feel envious of them.

CHAPTER V
New Month in Kentucky

Sunday, July 1, 1979

A new month has arrived, and we decided to hang out in Berea for the day, maybe get some riding done in the early evening in hopes of it being a little cooler. We spent most of the day exploring the campus of Berea College and pedaled around there until late afternoon. We departed town around 4:30pm and cycled west until 9:00 at night, pedaling a total of forty-five miles. The terrain is still hilly, but less so than previous parts of the Appalachians. I'm definitely looking forward to cycling on the flat stretches of Kansas, just shy of three states from here.

We sleep in a schoolyard tonight in Burgin, Kentucky. It is a clear night, so we pitch our tent and eat a cold dinner without making a fire. John examines the TransAmerica map with his flashlight determining that we are only four or five miles from Harrodsburg, a big town. We decided to stop in Harrodsburg for breakfast and plan our ride for the day.

Monday, July 2, 1979

We broke camp in the schoolyard arriving at Harrodsburg about 9:30 in the morning and stopped for breakfast at a Café. Over breakfast we discussed whether we should stay in town for tourist attractions like Fort Harrodsburg, or press on westward. John suggested we try for Hodgenville about sixty-five miles west and we agreed. We finished our breakfast exiting the Café to our bicycles making ready for the days trek.

We departed town between 10:00 and 10:30 and pedaled the rollercoaster hills to Springfield about the hallway mark where we decided to stop for lunch and a swim in the city pool. I called Patti to check on her and hear her voice again then stopped at a grocery to buy vegetables and cheese for lunch. We biked to a park in Springfield to eat our lunch and I wrote a letter to my brother Bill and his family. We had used most of the supplies John mailed to himself, yet there were more shipments to retrieve. Afterward, we cycled to the community pool had a refreshing swim, dried off, changed hanging the wet things on our panniers and I managed to mail my letter at the town Post Office before closing.

Departed Springfield at 4:30pm for the thirty-five-mile run to Hodgenville facing more rolling hills on Route 84. We were five miles shy of the town by 9 – 9:30pm when we met a Baptist Preacher and his wife on the front yard of their church. We stopped to chat, one thing led to another, and we were invited to spend the night in the church basement.

The Reverend and Mrs. Hadden were very hospitable and did not appear to be much older than us, as he was ten months completed with Ministry school and this was his first parish assignment. Reverend Hadden struck me as a devout and certainly quite enthusiastic minister, and he and his wife were a very sharing couple. They fixed us a hot meal for dinner and allowed us to use their shower before going to sleep in real beds. We slept in waking at about 10:30 in the morning when we hurried to pack the gear back on our bicycles. Mrs. Haden gave us each a bag of fresh baked cookies and we were off for Hodgenville.

Tuesday, July 3, 1979

We decided to stay over in Hodgenville and visit the birthplace of Abraham Lincoln in Kentucky. The area of Lincoln's birthplace is called Sinking Spring Farm named for a cool, clear spring on the 300-acre property. Abe was born to Tom and Sara Lincoln on February 12, 1809, in a one room cabin with a dirt floor. The cabin has been restored on the farm which is now a historical landmark. At the cabin site we spoke with a Park Guard who also worked as a history teacher in Kentucky. His name was Art and he told us in detail Lincoln's heritage as well as other historical facts about the State.

We left Hodgenville around 4:30pm hoping to make Rough River Dam State Park before nightfall. We pedaled forty-five miles through mostly hilly terrain, tired and achy we stopped to make camp at 7:30 at night. We picked a graveyard behind a small church to sleep too exhausted to pitch the tent, we just crashed in the tall grass with our sleeping bags. The thought was a graveyard would be a peaceful place to spend the night, but nothing could be further from the truth. Within minutes of us bedding down in the tall grass of the neglected graveyard a swarm of mosquitos, gnats, chiggers, no-see-ums, all and any assortment of biting midge attacked us ravaging every patch of bare flesh they could find.

The three of us rolled, smacked, and scratched in defense of the nights torment. I resorted to donning long pants and windbreaker with the hood up and all my exposed skin covered with Cutter's Woodsman repellant. Still, it was to no avail as the barrage of bites and ear-piercing buzzing persisted with no end. It was too humid to climb into my sleeping bag, so I crawled beneath my rain poncho for protection, but still the insect attack persisted. Eventually from sheer exhaustion I blanked out the torment from the biting, buzzing insects and began to doze.

Suddenly, I was awakened with my cycling mates by the rumble of thunder and lightning flashes then droplets began to fall gradually from the night sky. We rose from our sleeping positions and quickly erected the tent, crawling inside and out of the rain that now fell heavily through the darkness. I cannot speak for my fellow travelers, but I drifted off to sleep immediately and remained in slumberland for a few hours before dawn broke to awaken me.

Wednesday, July 4, 1979

The rain had cleared off with the new day, but the biting insects returned with a vengeance in this ill-kept place of the dead. So, we hurriedly broke camp packed up our bicycles and hightailed it from the graveyard as fast as we could pedal. We came upon a general store somewhere in Falls of Rough and decided to stop for breakfast. Inside the store we met a man and woman as proprietors, and the woman served sandwiches; the first general store on the trail that made deli-sandwiches and I felt like I was back in NY. Yet, when I took the first bite of mine, I realized they were a poor substitute for real delicatessen fare, a strange concoction that I call cheesed-ham sandwiches. So called as instead of using deli-ham and cheese slices they provided American cheese pressed into some kind of ham loaf, not the most appetizing of deli food, but we were more hungry than particular.

After we bought and ate our cheesed-ham sandwiches we asked the proprietors how far to reach Rough River Dam State Park and if they would have fireworks displayed at night? We were told the park was a mere twelve miles from their store and were likely to have a celebration for Independence Day. We left the general store for the park planning to stay there overnight and view the fireworks. The twelve-mile ride consisted of gradual, yet frequent hills to the park eventually passing over the Rough River Dam. The last five miles into the park bore steep and winding road like some of the switchbacks encountered in the Appalachians of Virginia.

We finally arrived at Rough River Dam Park and paid three dollars for a campsite, bicycled to it and setup our tents. I did not do much for the rest of the day, wrote postcards to Patti, some other friends, and read some of "At the Mountains of Madness" by H.P. Lovecraft, a paperback I brought along on the trip. I really enjoy the eerie stories written by this author and felt this title was a good choice to bring on the TransAmerica bicycle trip.

For dinner we sprung for a five dollar all you can eat buffet at the Park Resort Restaurant and gorged ourselves like it was a Thanksgiving feast. I believe I entered the buffet line five times counting each trip as one dollar towards the total amount to partake in the smorgasbord, but after five servings I felt so bloated as if to bust wide open. We hung around the resort digesting until 9:00pm when the fireworks were scheduled to start.

Within one hour prior to the fireworks a singing group performed, a mediocre ensemble calling themselves the Summer Sounds. The group consisted of eight members, one played piano while the others sang all the old favorite-unfavorites and acted out their songs in pantomime. A particularly pathetic performance was "Row, Row, Row Your Boat" as they sang the round in a forced, but dismal harmony and pretended to row invisible oars. Fortunately, their performance lasted less than one hour after which we walked to the shoreline to see the fireworks display over the man-made lake created by the dam.

The fireworks commenced at 9:00pm and lasted about fifteen minutes. It was a decent, but not sensational display with a standard barrage of rockets and ariel bombs. However, the show seemed to peter out at the end instead of finishing with a climatic explosion, which left most of the spectators wanting a bit more and we headed back to our camp a little disappointed.

Early the next day we awoke and met two teens on bicycles about fifteen years old who were just cycling within the State. They had ridden from Louisville to the Rough River State Park approximately one hundred and ten miles. I chatted with the youths for a while discovering that they arrived late yesterday afternoon a few hours after our entry into the park.

Thursday, July 5, 1979

John, Craig, and I pedaled out of the park at 1:00pm and cycled some undetermined mileage in the highland rim toward Whitesville and beyond on the TransAmerica trail. We took our bicycles over terrain containing a series of repetitive hills not offering much in scenery. We pedaled past a succession of fertile farmland featuring row upon row of crop like barley, tobacco, or corn that began to blur into unanimity of sameness, and I felt myself drift into a hypnotic state while riding my bicycle. My body numbed and I became oblivious to the sweat running down my head onto my glasses and into my ears.

Rail fencing bordered the road on both sides with occasional posting of "NO TRESPASSING" signs to keep interlopers and transients away from the acres of crop. I cycled slightly ahead of John and Craig transfixed in my daze of getting on, going forward, and reaching our next camp. I remembered John said we would try for the next camp in a town called Utica and we'd try to ride straight through with no breaks from Rough River State Park.

It was at dusk when the incident occurred that shattered the oblivion and brought me abruptly out of my summer daze. I was pedaling in the lead through the rolling hills in stretches of farmland when I heard a loud screech like a woman's scream that nearly knocked me off the seat of my ten-speed. I turned to see the source of the startling noise and found a peacock perched on a rail fence to my right. It dawned on me in that instance that some farmers' use peacocks to discourage trespassers and the beautiful fowl were as effective as barbed-wire, signs, or farm dogs.

At 7:00pm we were three miles outside of Utica, Kentucky, so we stopped at a general store to pickup some provisions for the night. The store was managed by a friendly woman named Irma. Irma was quite friendly in addition to accepting our purchase she gave us ice water, fresh bananas, and baked goods.

"Thank you for the extra provisions." I acknowledged and asked, "Do you know of a church in Utica that might offer us shelter for the night?"

"No, I'm sorry I don't." replied Irma, "but I have an unfurnished house that you're welcome to use, it's right across the street."

"That'll be Great!" John commented, "Thanks very much."

Irma escorted us to her house across from her store and showed us inside, it contained a stove, shower with hot water, and toilet, the electricity was on, and it even had air-conditioning. We immediately turned on the AC each of us showered and cooked ourselves a nice dinner. That night we slept better than we had in a long time with no biting bugs and no rain lying down in the dampness. The big plus was we had not slept in an air-conditioned room since Lexington and it was all due to kindly, old Irma. God Bless, Irma!

Friday, July 6, 1979

After breakfast we departed Irma's house around 8:30 in the morning pedaling through Utica and on into Sebree, Kentucky where we planned to stop for lunch. By 1:00pm we reached the small town of Sebree where I bought cottage cheese and vegetables for lunch at a grocery store. The main street through town reminded me of something you might see in the Old West with simple wooden structures all built close together in a neat little community.

We met a Minister outside the grocery and got to talking with him. He introduced himself as Reverend True of the Christian Church of God and commenced in giving us some detail on his town. It seems the town was named for Col. E.G. Sebree, Mining Company Owner and President who helped bring the railroad into the area. Reverend True went on to tell us that the town had fallen on hard times since the days Sebree was around and most of the town-folk were starving for work or had the hard and often futile occupation of working a farm.

"We use to have a lot of coal mining round these parts," the Reverend pointed out, "but now a days the mines aren't hardly worked at all. Well, a whole lotta folks moved on and those that haven't are just starving for work.

"I figure the average age of townsfolk here is bout sixty-five. Yes, we got a man in the Marathon building over there cross the street whose seventy and still workin' a forty-hour-week. He's one of the lucky ones with work while many are unemployed, elderly, but they still want to work. Sure wish Mr. Carter would take a look at our situation and do somthin' bout it."

We listened intently to the Minister's complaining while eating our lunches then Craig politely asked if there was a community pool in town.

He answered that there was and directed us to its location. The three of us mounted our bicycles and followed Reverend True's directions. Along the way we passed some younger boys walking from the opposite direction.

"Hey!" Hollered one of the boys, "You goin' to the pool?"

John answered loudly from his bike, "Yes."

"Well, don't bother," another boy remarked, "cause it's closed."

We froze in mid-stride on our bicycles in disappointment and decided to press on to Marion, Kentucky the last town enroute before reaching the State's border. John had sent himself a food package at the Post Office in Marion and I had arranged for some new bicycle tires to be shipped there from home. We reached the small town of Dixon at 3:30pm and took another break after about an hour then kicked out the last twenty-five miles to Marion. Unfortunately, by the time we arrived the Post Office was closed, so we sat in front of the Courthouse deciding what to do.

Eventually, we were approached by an old man who stopped to chat with us for a while. The old fellow appeared to be in his sixties, still in fairly good shape and he began to reminisce about the good old days when he used to sit in his truck drinking corn liquor, get too drunk to drive home.

"Yeah," he said with a sigh, "that was about sixty years back."

"Well, you must've been around ten." remarked Craig with a smile, "because you don't look much older than sixty."

"Shoot son," quipped the old gentleman, "I'm eighty years old and my Momma didn't allow me to drink when I was a child. Yeah, I'm eighty and lived here all my life. Use-ta' have a farm like my Daddy before me, but I sold off three hundred acres of good bottom land back in the sixties and haven't worked a day since.

John asked him if he knew of a place in town where we could sleep?

To which he replied, "Shoot, I already told you more than I know, but you might try the waterworks bout a mile outta town."

Following his direction and we found the waterworks, but an employee there told us we were not permitted to sleep on the premises. He told us that there was a lake park about one mile further that was better suited for camping, so we pressed on. The mile of road ahead of us was covered in heavy gravel that made bicycling quite difficult forcing us to dismount and walk our bikes to the park. We arrived in the dark exhausted and discouraged and fell asleep in our bags set on top of picnic tables having traveled some seventy miles today.

Saturday, July 7, 1979

We awoke to a hazy and humid morning packed up our sleeping bags and walked our bicycles to rideable pavement pedaling back to Marion from there. Back in town we ate a good breakfast and went to the Post Office to pick up our parcels. John collected the food package and I got my new bicycle tires, which I immediately mounted on my Schwinn tossing the old, bald ones away in the trash. I arranged for my parents to mail me a care package at the Marion Post Office that would include the bicycle tires. John's food package consisted of some dry goods like macaroni meals and several packages of freeze-dried meals designed for backpackers. There was enough food in the parcel to last us a week, maybe more and John mailed himself several of these along the route. This was his third pick up.

After I mounted my new tires, the haze turned into a steady drizzle of rain so we waited around town to see if it would subside, and it cleared off by noontime. We left Marion for the Ohio River and arrived at (La Belle Riviere) the beautiful river at 1:00pm. We took a ferryboat across the Ohio at Cave-in-Rock State Park in Illinois for lunch. I was glad to leave Kentucky with her attacking farm dogs, Billie-goats, and noisy peacocks. Although we had met some friendly people like Irma, Rhonda, and the unusual bicycle-hitchhiking trio. Still, I was looking forward to cycling the roads in Illinois bordered by the two great rivers.

CHAPTER VI
Over the River to Illinois

At Cave-in-Rock we met a guy and two girls, all three were law students on a weekend vacation. The six of us explored the natural attraction as a group discovering that it was hollowed out by the Ohio River wash and used as a hideout by river bandits where they would lure and kill hostages after robbing them. As we explored the cave and read of its history on the posted signs I kept thinking about "The Rivers" segment in "How the West was Won" that featured Jimmy Stewart, Karl Malden, and Walter Brennan among others. Walter Brennan portrayed a sly old river pirate that came vividly back to me as we explored the cave.

After touring the cave John, Craig, and I set out for Eddyville planning to camp in the Shawnee National Forest. The terrain was hilly and we traveled on Route 146 to avoid a thirty-six-mile stretch of gravel road. We stopped at a small church to rest along 146 where we met a couple restoring a statue of Christ. We spoke to the couple while drinking from our water bottles, refilled them with fresh water at the church's pump and started off again. A few miles further brought us to Eddyville Road, a long stretch of blacktop with a few very steep climbs. We arrived in the town of Eddyville just shy of nightfall pedaling up to the Route 145 intersection where we asked a general store proprietor direction to a campsite.

The proprietor told us to continue on 145 and make our first left-hand turn and we would find a small camp on the road. Our trio followed his direction and headed north on 145 for about one mile stopping at a package store for something to eat and more direction. Parking our bicycles outside, we entered the store purchasing chips and beer.

Two attractive girls were working the counter, but we were too tired to flirt and only interested in finding a place to sleep. John asked them for directions to the camp since he was buying the beer and was told that there was a campsite up the road, but it was up a two-mile gravel run. We did not look forward to walking our bicycles up a gravel road in the dark, so we asked if there were any churches near by to camp at. One of the girls suggested we try the community center back in Eddyville since people sleep there sometimes.

We thanked the girls for the information took our purchase and exited the package store. We packed the beer and chips on our bicycles, pedaled back into Eddyville and found the community center adjacent to the Director's house after asking for more directions in town. The three of us went to the Director's house and knocked on the door to ask to stay at the community center.

A middle-aged man sporting a bushy moustache answered the door with a smile an introduced himself as Ralph Aly Community Center Director, Funeral Director, and Mayor of Eddyville. He was very friendly and offered us a shower, some beer and barbecue sandwiches, and his backyard for camping instead of the unfurnished community center. We gladly accepted his offer and set our sleeping bags on lounge chairs in his backyard after which we each took turns using his shower in the house. We placed our beer in a large cooler our host had in his yard and partook of the delicious barbecue sandwiches he offered.

Ralph Aly explained to us over some drinking and eating that he held a big party here on the Fourth to view the fireworks display. "We went through a couple of kegs of beer and three sides of barbecue beef before the evening was over."

The talking went on for hours until the mayor finally called it an evening. "Shoot, the talk's been as rich as a foot up a bull's ass." Mayor Aly announced rising from a lounge chair, "Time I turned in, goodnight boys."

John, Craig, and I agreed, bid our host goodnight, and fell asleep almost immediately due to the day's exhaustive cycling and mass consumption of beer. I slept soundly with my sleeping bag on a lounge chair, which was almost as comfortable as laying on a bed. I awoke bright and cheerful the next morning free of biting insects, dampness from rain and best of all void of the oppressive humidity.

Sunday, July 8, 1979

We pedaled approximately fifty-five miles from Cave-in-Rock to Eddyville and as Mayor Aly was so hospitable, we decided to make a relaxing slow start before going on. Mayor Aly invited us to attend church with him and Craig accepted immediately. John and I were a little more hesitant as we did not have any clean slacks to wear, but the mayor assured us that would not be a problem.

We took showers, changed into fresh riding clothes, and piled into Ralph Aly's station wagon as he drove off to his church. We arrived in time for the 10:00am service and I was happy to see that the church was a Methodist denomination as that was mine as well. I sat in the pew with John, Craig and Mayor Aly singing the old hymnals as loudly and faithfully as I could.

Our TransAmerica trio was warmly welcomed by the Minister and his congregation despite our inappropriate dress. The Minister even mentioned us a few times during his sermon. After the service Mayor Aly drove us back to his house where we packed our bicycle panniers and thanked him for his gracious hospitality. We got on our bikes and pedaled onto Carbondale a sixty-mile distance from Eddyville.

After reaching Route 147 we pedaled through the town of Simpson and came upon two steep climbs. The humidity felt heavy at this point of the day that made pedaling over the rises even tougher to accomplish. When we passed those two climbs it was time to take a break, so we stopped in front of Bradley's Saw Filing and Repair Shop. An elderly man was working out in the front yard of the establishment, who I assumed to be Mr. Bradley. John asked him for some water, and he gave us access to his well kept clean with purification tablets.

We resumed the bike trip after resting at Bradley's place bicycling onto Tunnel Hill Road that brought us to the town of the same name and beyond. We stopped again in Goreville for a quick lunchbreak and discovered we were about twentyfive-miles from Carbondale. Goreville appeared practically deserted probably due to the Sunday afternoon presuming the Blue Laws were in force. Nothing was open and hardly anyone was out on Main Street except for a few locals buzzing around on motorcycles. A sizeable group of bikers were hanging out in a gas station lot, which was also closed and of course we were there, but no one else. We ate our snack lunches sitting at a bus stop bench then mounted our bicycles and continued onto Carbondale, Illinois arriving at 5:30pm.

In Carbondale our cycling trio found a pizza place open, so we stopped there for dinner. The pizza was a little expensive over $2.00 a slice, but we figured we could pay outrageous pizza prices instead of gas prices. After all the pizza was to us like gas was to a car, the fuel providing mobility. Despite the cost the slices were quite good, thick crusted and tasty Sicilian pizza.

After our dinner we departed the over-priced eatery and stood outside getting the lay of the land in this Illinois college town. Suddenly, a medical student happened by, noticed our touring bikes, and offered us a place to stay if nothing else turned up. He gave us his dorm address on campus, and we told him that we would more than likely be by later. We walked our bikes over to a nearby laundromat after meeting the med. student and unpacked our dirty clothes. While doing our laundry we received two more offers for a place to stay, one from a broadcast student who broadcasted a campus news show and the second offer from a graduate of the college. The broadcast student mentioned that he would like to interview us on his college radio show, and we agreed to his request.

That night we stayed with the broadcast student named Mark and he resided in a trailer-home near the campus, but after doing our laundry we went to a local bar with the graduate by the name of Mike Robey. Mike lived in a rented house approximately six miles outside of town and since he also offered us a place to crash, we decided to stay in Carbondale for two days. We arranged to stay at Mark's place tonight and Mike's tomorrow night.

The five of us (Mike, Mark and our trio) went to the bar after the laundromat and we all tied one on. While drinking a mug of beer I noticed two or three pool tables at the rear of the bar and a large sign that read: The Home of Minnesota Fats. I asked Mike about the sign, and he informed me that Fats got his start hustling pool in this very bar, pool hall. Around 10:00pm we left Mike at the bar for SIU (Southern Illinois University) to the radio station so Mark could arrange for our interview then hiked to his trailer where we camped out in our sleeping bags.

Monday, July 9, 1979

Our sleep in the trailer was interrupted by a fierce electrical storm, I eventually fell back asleep and awoke with the others at 8:00am. We showered and ate breakfast in a hurry then rushed over to the college radio station for our interview. The interview went quite well with Mark asking each of us questions about our trip and where we were from. I even told him about the goat attack in Kentucky and the screaming assault by the watch-peacock on the rail fence.

After the interview Craig toured the campus on his bicycle while John and I located a bicycle repair shop, the internationally famous, "Bike Surgeon" where we spent some money on bicycle upgrades. We replaced our rear wheel gear clusters for lower gear ratios hoping that would improve our pedaling over the Ozark mountains that lay ahead of us. In retrospect I think the gear ratio change did little to improve my cycling ability, more of a psychological edge rather than a physical one, much like discarding my kickstand in Wytheville to lessen the weight of my bicycle. However, I made the gear ratio change with John and told myself that the pedals turned so much easier in low gear.

Later that day we met two more cyclists heading west on the TransAmerica trail with the names Mike and Greg out of Milwaukie. We agreed to meet them tomorrow morning at the bike store and ride on together. We connected back up with Craig on the SIU campus and cranked it out to Mike Robey's house arriving there by 6:00pm. It just started to rain hard when we departed Carbondale, which was just our luck since we were soaking wet when we arrived at Mike's place.

Mike warm heartedly invited us in and fixed us a fresh fish dinner, but forgot to scale the fish before cooking it in the oven. I guess Mike Robey was not used to preparing fresh fish dinners, so we ended up peeling the baked skin off to eat the meat beneath. The fish was delicious despite the additional work to eat the meal. After dinner Mike took Craig and I on a bar crawl while John stayed back to get some rest.

We drifted into three different drinking establishments as Mike looked for his housemate, a fellow by the name of Nate Nobey. Oddly enough, Mike Robey shared a house with Nate Nobey. It would have been a perfect ternate of rhymes if Mr. Robey and Mr. Nobey lived in an Adobe. Alas, this was not the case as Mike and Nate were simply housemates with a cadence in their sir names. I kept these poetic thoughts to myself as I drank a few beers in each bar.

After we crawled through the three bars and I consumed the equivalent of a rack of beer, Mike still did not locate Nate. Finally, he gave up and in depressed regret Mike decided to return home with Craig and I in tow. We walked into his living room and found Nate Nobey sitting with John watching television. Mike dragged us on a bar crawl for two to three hours searching for his housemate to find him at last sitting in their house.

I do not believe I spoke a single word to Nate Nobey, as he sat silently watching tv. I did greet him to say hello after Mike introduced us, but no other words were passed in conversation. I found it curious that our host hardly spoke to his housemate aside from greeting him when we entered the living room and making introductions for Craig and myself. It was indeed unusual if not freakishly ironic that Mike spent his time while showing us the nightlife of Carbondale, searching for the elusive Nate Nobey, only to fall mostly silent when confronting him in their shared residence. I got to bed late in the night but slept like a top under the daze of several draft beers.

Tuesday, July 10, 1979

Our TransAm trio got on the road around 8:00 in the morning and pedaled back to Carbondale after saying goodbye to Mike and thanking him for letting us stay at his house. The rainfall had ceased from last night and the morning seemed somewhat cleared off so we arrived at the Bike Surgeon Shop in about fifteen to twenty minutes. We waited and waited, but the cyclists from Milwaukie were nowhere to be seen. Finally, we departed Carbondale at 9:00am as we had arrived a cycling threesome.

Stopped for lunch in a little town called Ava, Illinois where John and I whipped up a big salad. After eating we hung around Ava for an hour or two and digested then got on the road to the Mississippi River and the Illinois, Missouri border. We were approximately forty miles from our destination.

It must have taken us over four hours to cover that ground because it was 7:00pm when we reached the banks of the mighty Mississippi River. Bad road conditions of mostly gravel and broken pavement in conjunction of sweltering humidity made the going slow. The last ferry had departed for the other side at 5:00pm, so we began to look for a place to stay in Chester.

We pedaled back some four miles and a fellow by the name of Roger offered his backyard for us to make camp, we gladly took him up on his offer. Roger, his family, and friends threw a party in the yard surrounding our campsite and provided plenty of beer for the occasion. While participating in the party John noticed two cyclists pedaling down the street approaching the party and our campsite.

"Damn, I don't believe it." John exclaimed, "Greg and Mike from Milwaukee are here."

We drank and talked and drank some more, getting better acquainted. Mike called Greg, Stinky and Greg's nickname for Mike was Jingles on account of the noise his keychain made when he pedaled. Henceforth I will refer to our new co-cyclists on the TransAmerica trail as Stinky and Jingles. Roger got out his guitar and began to play, so I accompanied him on my juice-harp that I carried with me everywhere. We jammed and drank and made more music which suffered miserably from our drinking and finally we were both too tired to strum and twang. It was quite late when we got to sleep, and I was stinking drunk again.

Wednesday, July 11, 1979

We woke up early and I arose with a dreaded beer hangover from too much partying last night. Stinky broke a spoke and John helped him make repairs truing the wheel while Craig and I rode ahead to check out the Big Muddy in daylight. The river did not meet my expectations. In fact, I was somewhat disappointed upon first sight of this historical waterway. True to her nickname the Mississippi was very, very muddy and I could not bring myself to be excited by this brown, cloudy expanse of water. Adventurous fantasies of Old Man River and Huck Finn with Big Jim rafting her watercourse faded into the reality of the Big Muddy.

Eventually, John, Stinky, and Jingles joined us at the riverbank where Craig and I waited for the ferryboat, it was 9:00am. The ferry was on the Missouri side of the river and when it crossed it brought two more cyclists on an eastbound tour of the TransAmerica trail. We chatted with them a short while as the ferryboat refueled for the voyage back across the Big Muddy. The cyclists told us they were from San Francisco and planned to bike all the way down to Miami then the Keyes. We asked them about the roads ahead and told them that they would need protection from farm dogs through Kentucky, as I flashed my snakewhip.

They thanked us for the heads-up on the dogs remarking that there was not any problem with them going west. They did warn us of the Ozarks through Missouri and stretches of nothingness in Kansas, but we did look forward to pedaling some real flat ground. I had not seen a long flat stretch since John, and I departed Long Island and I almost forgot what it was like to bicycle without being challenged by rollercoaster climbs.

The ferryboat finished fueling so we boarded with our bicycles and crossed Tom and Huck's playground. It was about noontime when we arrived in downtown Ste. Genevieve, Missouri. We stopped at a bakery to nosh a lunch of pastries. This was the first bakeshop I encountered on the trip thus far and the pastries were delicious. We stood in front of the bakery eating pastries when a man walked up to us.

He introduced himself as Steve and told us that he lived next store to the bakery in a one-room-flat. Steve noticed our grunge from cycling and sleeping outdoors, and offered us the use of his shower, all five of us eagerly accepted. I am not sure if Steve realized that five, grimy cyclists would use his shower, one after another, because when we were done the shower was probably drained of hot water and looked grungier than us prior to its use.

There were scant furnishings in Steve's flat. All I saw was a table with a tambourine set upon it, a chair, and a cot for a bed. I saw no kitchen utility or even a television and I thought that maybe the tambourine was his means of earning income. Our group of five thanked Steve for the use of the shower and departed his one-room-flat around 3:30pm. Since it was late in the day and we had just showered we decided not to do any extensive bicycling and stay in the city park that night. We purchased groceries for dinner and pedaled to the camp area of the park. There we met two more eastbound cyclists, spoke with them for a bit over dinner and beer, and headed to bed early for a change.

Our passage through Illinois went quite smoothly and quickly having bicycled from the Ohio to the Old Miss in three full days of pedaling. As in Virginia and Kentucky, our group met some hospitable folks across the states we traveled up to the arrival in Ste. Genevieve. Ralph Aly of Eddyville was surely the nicest person met so far and certainly a good talker. He probably won the mayoral election in Eddyville by a landslide.

While resting in Ste. Genevieve I noticed a Merchants Bank / Ste. Genevieve Savings Bank Marker located on the corner of Merchant Street and South Main Street, which was the location of the old bank. The marker had a photograph of the bank as well as some historical facts about the building, where a gas station now stood. The building was erected in 1837 and torn down for a Standard Oil Gas Station in 1934. Five members of the James Gang entered Ste. Genevieve with the intent to rob the Ste. Genevieve Savings Bank (previously known as the Merchant's Bank) on May 27, 1873. They escaped with about $4,100, much of it in silver. I wondered at what point in Jesse James's bank robbing career this heist took place?

CHAPTER VII

Across the Big Muddy in Missouri

Thursday, July 12, 1979

We awoke in the park at 8:00am to discover the eastbound cyclists were leaving to catch the ferry crossing the Mississippi. It began to rain as we packed our gear onto our bicycles, so we decided to wait awhile before starting out as it was a bitch riding on our bikes being pelted by rain. We rode out of the park when the downpour let up a little and stopped for breakfast at a restaurant downtown in Ste. Genevieve.

After breakfast the five of us mounted our bicycles and pedaled out of town at 10:30am. By 12:30pm we made Farmington, Missouri and decided to break for lunch. Our group pedaled to a graveyard in town where John broke out some of the food, he mailed to himself, and we heated it with water over a camping stove Stinky carried in his panniers. After lunch we lounged in the graveyard digesting while John planned our destination for the day.

In reflection of our bicycle trek, I must admit that we rested at quite a few graveyards along the way. It may have been a subconscious effort of our young group celebrating our mortality, or we were simply drawn to the peacefulness and tranquility of the resting places of those souls departed. Regardless of the reason morbid, or otherwise graveyards became our preferred choice to take a break.

Now, these many years later I often boast that on my cross-country trek in 79, I slept everyplace except a jail. I have made my bed in abandoned houses, backyards, camps, churches, churchyards and sometimes in the peacefulness of graveyards, but never have I been spooked by a ghost.

After digesting in the tranquil graveyard, we mounted our bicycles for the Johnson's Shut-In State Park. We got our first real taste of cycling in the Ozarks, and I have to say that the taste was not one I desired. The Ozarks offered us several steep climbs, but unlike those in the Appalachians these inclines went straight up. Climbing the Ozarks on bicycle in a way was easier than pedaling the Appalachians, as you at least could see your goal at the top of a rise. Where as in the switchback runs through Appalachia the roads carried you in a swirl and as you turned a bend hoping to see the crest of a mountain route, your hopes were continually dashed in the continuation of a climb.

It was the agony of those zigzag inclines through Virginia, West Virginia, and Kentucky that gave me the occasional inclination to toss my bicycle and catch a bus back to the flatness of Long Island. However, the ecstasy of rolling into a spiraling downhill like what we found on Afton Mountain always made me excited to be on this adventure. Admittedly those moments on my Schwinn Superior on the first leg of the TransAmerica trail were second only to the rapture of sexual pleasure. Anyone who has flown down a mountain descent carried by two one and one-quarter inch wheels with gusts dancing in your hair and ears like the constant gale in a wind tunnel understands my comparison.

John and I resumed our five-minute rest for every hour of cycling as a model for the rest of the group. After several climbs in the Ozarks covering sixty-five miles, we arrived at the Shut-Ins Park in Middle Brook, Missouri. It was 7:00 at night when we got our camp set-up, so John and I took a swim before darkness fell upon us. Our campsite was close to the park office and swimming was available on the east fork of the Black River approximately one-quarter mile away on a paved trail. We removed the panniers from our bikes and pedaled down to east fork of the river with towels around our necks.

The swim area was still occupied with a few swimmers despite the late hour. We watched some teenage boys hurling themselves off high cliffs of volcanic rock into deep pools of water from the Black River. Initially Jon and I simply waded into the whitewater that funneled through the gorge of the east fork. After awhile we got a little bolder and jumped from cliffs rising some ten feet above the river flow. Neither of us dared to leap from the higher precipice used by the teenagers, as we were uncertain of the layout of the gorge's bottom and did not wish to turn the leisurely swim into a tragic, broken bone event.

John figured the high cliffs were about fifty feet above the water and that seemed like a reasonable assessment given their height in relation to the ones from which we took our jumps, Both John and I watched the nervy teens jump one after another from the high volcanic perch into the algae-green water showing no fear. While we shrank at the thought of attempting the feat boldly demonstrated by the fearless youths, our enthusiasm to jump from the ten-foot-high rock quickly diminished. After making a few more jumps into the refreshing pools provided by the Black River, we returned to camp and found Craig, Stinky and Jingles preparing dinner.

After dinner we cleaned up the pots and plates used for cooking and eating and packed away our goods on our bicycle panniers. Darkness fell upon us at the ShutIns as if a black blanket was thrown over our heads, so John and I lit the lanterns that we carried with us. The five of us strolled from our camp to a scenic overlook at the park and viewed countless stars illuminating the night. We dimmed our lanterns to the verge of being extinguished to fully appreciate the cosmic glow above us. I had never seen a star filled night sky as spectacular as this back on Long Island. Every constellation brightly shining in the darkness as far as the eye could see with a grandeur making our existence seem insignificant.

We sat and admired the stars in the sky at the scenic overlook for quite a while, eventually heading back to our camp. We crawled into our tents and fell asleep easily after the long day of bicycling the Ozarks. I remember hearing the noises of more campers arriving in the park prior to drifting into unconsciousness. The park entrance closed at 10:00pm so I must have dropped off before then since the last thing I heard were cars driving by our camp.

Friday, July 13, 1979

We awoke early, but did not leave the park before noon the designated checkout time. We informed the park office that we would be leaving at 12:00pm as they assigned our campsite to another group bicycling the TransAmerica trail. Shortly before leaving the park two cyclists pulled up to use the camp: Jack from Pennsylvania and Bill from Kansas cycling east on the trail. We chatted with the new arrivals briefly then departed the park on Route 106 heading west.

It was a perfect day for bad luck as Stinky got a flat and Jingles broke a spoke on his front wheel. Of course, the mishaps occurred at different times during the day's ride and the heat, humidity, and mountainous terrain made the cycling tough in addition to the bicycle breakdowns. So, we gladly stuck to our regiment of five minutes rest for every hour of pedaling. By late afternoon we arrived at Ellington, Missouri and met four other cyclists going in the opposite direction. First, we ran across a pair of young women from Marin County, California then met a man and woman from Kansas. The couple from Kansas had their bicycles outfitted with homemade panniers that looked as good as my store-bought Bellwether brand, but not as nice as John's Cannondales.

We stayed on Route 106 the entire day and reached Owl's Bend Campground about 8:30 at night. After a series of rolling hills, we entered a descent of about two miles that led us straight into the campground. The downhill run refreshed me, but seemed a bit spooky in the darkness while our wheels spun in the black of night all you saw was a few feet of pavement in front of you illuminated by the glow of moonlight. When we arrived in the campground an old fellow adjacent to our assigned campsite offered us some baked beans. I got to talking with an elderly couple camping opposite to us and went to sleep late in the night.

Saturday, July 14, 1979

We broke camp and departed Owl's Bend early around 7:30 am and immediately hit that sweet two mile downhill in reverse. We labored up the steep incline out of the campground and the sun was already beating down on us even though it was early morning. Jingles broke another spoke shortly after we got started giving us a chance to bake in the heat and sweat from the stifling humidity without any shade for cover. After the better part of one-half-hour the spoke was replaced, wheel trued, and tire remounted with tube reinflated. We got on the road again and caught a slight break from the heat with the breeze created by our forward motion.

Our first real rest stop was taken in the town of Eminence, Missouri a nice little village where we relaxed for about ten minutes. As we entered the town, we passed a sign the read: WELCOME STAY A DAY OR A LIFETIME IN SHANNON CO. We later discovered that (Stay a Day or a Lifetime) was the town motto of Eminence. John took time during the stopover to get his bearings on the trail map for our next destination, Alley Spring State Park. Our good fortune was that Alley Spring turned out to be quite close to Eminence, but the route in-between contained more grueling hills with the repetitive straight upward climbs and deep valley descents.

We made Alley Spring by lunchtime, and I was the first in our group to enter the park. The spring called to me in its beauty forming a large pool of crystalline water surrounded by steep cliffs. The pool so clear that one could see water foliage growing from its rocky bottom. Beyond the spring stood Alley Mill, a picturesque red three-story structure that strikes you as vaguely familiar likely seen in oil paintings capturing a country place of tranquility. I felt very happy to be in this park quickly dismounted my Schwinn Superior leaping into the crystal-clear water of the spring anticipating a refreshing relief from the deadening heat and humidity.

Instead of relief I felt aghast. The icy mountain spring water struck my flesh like a million needles that abruptly shocked my body to a point of numbness. Within seconds of hitting the water I began to hyperventilate feeling my heart pound so fiercely as if it were to burst from my chest. I felt myself slipping into useless panic and nearly blacked out from shock, yet I struggled to retain consciousness swimming frantically to the opposite bank of the pool. Upon climbing out of Alley Spring I found a man tending a fire beneath a large still, a big copper vat that stood about four-foot tall with heavy copper tubing coiled around the top.

"Could've told ya," remarked the man, "not to do that. A young fella did the very same thang a week ago. Yes-sir, the Paramedics had to come and take him away."

"So, why didn't you stop me?" I asked, "Why did you let me jump in?

"Just wanted to see if those Paramedics were gonna come in here again," he replied with a laugh, "but I guess not. You look to be okay to me."

I watched the man stoke the fire with a billow and asked, "Is this a whiskey still?"

"Sure is," he proudly answered, "makes the finest corn liquor you'll find in the county."

John and the others arrived, stopping where I was talking to the man at the still while I retrieved my bicycle on the other bank of the spring. John questioned me on how I came to be soaked and I explained that I foolishly jumped into the spring, almost died climbed out to find this gentleman distilling corn whiskey. The man explained that he used to moonshine, got caught by the revenuers and made a deal with the judge to operate his still on weekends as a park exhibit. With three barrels of mash, his large still pot, thumper keg and condenser the moonshiner claimed to produce three gallons of 80% pure, kickass corn whiskey.

We each asked for a taste of his finished product, and he refused us offering instead a sampling of his mash. We looked at the corn slop in the barrels with flies lazing on their surfaces and declined his offer. Again, we pleaded for a taste of the real stuff, and he relented giving us each a small portion in a tin cup. I gulped mine quickly and it went down my gullet with a fiery sensation like a sip of lava flow cooking my insides.

I swallowed, gagged in reaction, and asked, "You make three gallons of this a day, what do you do with it?"

"Oh, I drink some," he answered, and feed the rest to my hogs. The law don't allow me to sell it no more, only get to display my moonshinin' for the tourists."

I was certain the moonshiner did not feed his product to the hogs maybe the corn slop, but not that white lightening. If what he answered was true then he owned the happies hogs in the county. All of us sampled the moonshiner's goods and hung around the park for lunch then headed out for Summerville, Missouri to make camp for the night.

We continued on Route 106 for about twenty miles reaching Summerville in a few hours making camp in the town park. A local Patrol car pulled into the park carrying two policemen who granted us permission to camp there shortly after we arrived. We conversed with the policemen for a while, and they informed us that there was a bluegrass band performing in the Café across the street that night. After dinner we strolled over to be entertained by live music. We indulged in some beer drinking and after I hoisted a few I took out my juice-harp and joined in with the band. After forty-five miles of hard cycling this was a fitting end of the day.

CHAPTER VIII
Finishing off the Ozarks

Sunday, July 15, 1979

Today, John realized we weren't too much further from Lazy Louie's Bicycle Camp a retreat for cyclists highlighted in the accompanying camping guides to the Bikecentennial maps. Apparently, Lazy Louie (Louis Schultz) like the Cookie Lady in Virginia established himself as a haven of hospitality for cyclists traveling the trail through Missouri. We packed up our gear and biked about twenty miles to the town of Houston and stopped for a late breakfast.

First John stopped at the town Post Office to pick-up another shipment of food then we found a Diner on Main Street to order our breakfast. Here we met two fellow cyclists from Amsterdam, the Netherlands; Paul and Phillip who began their tour in Astoria, Oregon. We ate breakfast with these two, sitting at a table for seven and enthusiastically swapping our experiences on the bicycle adventure. The Dutchmen told us about Lazy Louie's camp having stayed there and guessed it was about forty or fifty miles from Houston.

This was the only real break we took all day the rest was hard pedaling in eagerness of reaching Lazy Louie's place. We stopped at a roadside creek for a refreshing dip in the cool water ate a quick lunch then made for Hartville, Missouri. This brought us roughly ten miles east of Lazy Louie's and for the last leg I pedaled like a mad man on an exercise cycle, chanting to myself, "L-o-u-i-e, L-o-u-i-e, L-o-u-i-e, L-o-u-i-e." in rhythm to my stride on the Schwinn.

Finally, we arrived at Lazy Louie's Bicycle Camp and met the kind host to cyclists. Louie is a good old boy and hardly what I would call lazy as he maintained a large garden that provided Louie and his wife with most of their dietary needs. This led me to believe that his moniker was a misnomer, or maybe it referred to Louie's manner of speech that stretched out in a long lazy drawl commonly spoken in the deep south. However, Louie was from parts north of the Mason-Dixon Line, born some sixty-seven years ago in the Hawkeye State.

Louie told us, "I'm from I-oh-way."

Louie greeted our arrival with some ice cold well water and a warm smile. The campsite costs us one dollar a night and Louie offered us showers for another buck, which we accepted without hesitation. Before, during and after dinner Louie sat and chatted with us, an amiable old fellow recapping his growing up in "I-oh-way" and later moving here to "Miz-or-rah." We never met Mrs. Schultz, but Louie stayed on and chewed the fat well into the night.

John asked if our host would favor us with some songs and guitar playing described in the TransAmerica trail guidebook as "Lazy Louie's Easy Listening Music." He declined to get out his guitar for a live performance but offered a self-recorded audio tape for ten dollars. John purchased one tape from our kindly host to play when he returned home.

Louie claimed that he was playing the guitar for most of his life since he learned to make chords back in 23' and boasted that he could play fourteen instruments in all. However, he refused to demonstrate his musical talent regardless of how much we pleaded for him to do so. I did get a chance to hear some of Lazy Louie's Easy Listening Music on the audio tape that John spent ten dollars to acquire. It was many months later back in Amityville when John and I got together, and he played his cassette for me. Louie's songs were fair for a home recording, but certainly would not go gold in sales and I was glad I did not buy that tape when I had a chance.

Shortly before Louie retired for the evening another cyclist going west on the trail arrived at the camp traveling solo in our direction. John, I and the others in our group thought it odd that this fellow pedaled into Lazy Louie's all by himself in the dead of night. After Louie retreated to his house, we washed up our dishes and cooking utensils from dinner, and setup our camp with cots that Louie provided. Craig, Stinky and Jingles turned in for the night while John and I talked with the new arrival.

His name was Jim and stated he came from Tennessee. Jim planned to go all the way to Oregon and bragged he was cycling the whole trail on two hundred dollars. When we asked him how he would manage to make the cross-country trek with such a small amount of cash?

He answered; "By livin' on peanut butter sandwiches and good old roadkill, but it gotta be fresh."

Jim carried a plastic bag on the back of his bicycle atop his panniers and when he spotted a "fresh" roadkill along the bike route, he scrapped it up and loaded into his bag. That evening he would skin out the flattened animal and cook it up for dinner. Fortunately, Jim did not acquire any fresh roadkill prior to his arrival at Lazy Louie's so ate his backup peanut butter sandwich for dinner.

Jim gave me a creepy feeling and I did not sleep very soundly that night even though I had the comfort of a cot. I eventually drifted off after worrying about the strangely morbid, loaner Jim joining our tour group's trek on the Bikecentennial trail. Admittedly, the thought of Jim scraping up the remains of a smooshed muskrat, opossum, or racoon from the road and stuffing it into his plastic trash bag later to skin-out, cook and eat turned into nightmare images as I slept. I normally do not remember my dreams the next day, but the pictured thoughts of the ghoulish, Tennessee Jim struck in me with night-terrors that were recalled in the morning.

I heard that Lazy Louie passed away in 1988 and I am sure he has a special place in Heaven. He is probably keeping the Almighty entertained with his Easy Listening Music.

Monday, July 16, 1979

We departed Lazy Louie's Bicycle Camp around 10:30 in the morning. Much to our relief, Jim decided to remain at the camp for another day and rest up before hitting the trail. Earlier that morning John and I filled the others in on Jim's unusual means of bicycling cross-country. None of our group of five felt comfortable cycling with Jim after discovering his morbid method of low budget bicycling on the trail and were quite glad when he decided to remain at the camp. John offered Jim two packages of freeze-dried food before we departed, and he accepted them with thanks.

I wondered if Jim was going to make it all the way to Oregon while living on peanut butter sandwiches and roadkill. I also wondered if I was going to make it to the west coast myself and be able to settle in California. I began to have doubts as my current funds were at two hundred dollars and I had no desire to resort to eating roadkill like Tennessee Jim.

As we pedaled away from Louie's once again in the hilly terrain of the Ozarks, I contemplated ways to make my money last all the way to California. Maybe I could break away from John and the group to work as a hired hand on a farm for a few weeks and earn a little money. Maybe I could borrow from my folks? No, neither Mom or Dad would go for that since I left Patti pregnant on her own while I went on my bicycle adventure.

We bicycled for fifteen miles on Route 38 since departing the camp and stopped in Marshfield, Missouri and meandered in town for about two hours before moving on. John reviewed the maps suggesting we try for Greenfield to make camp for the night. At 1:00 pm we pedaled out of Marshfield traveling about twenty miles to the town of Fair Grove where we were delayed a few more hours by a heavy rainfall. It finally let up and we pressed on at 5:30pm.

Making Greenfield late in the day was out of the question as the town was more than fifty miles away through hilly terrain. So, we opted for the town of Walnut Grove, another thirty-five miles through the Ozark heights from our present location. Shortly after departing Fair Grove, we came across a washed-out bridge where we portaged our bicycles through knee-high water. A hairy circumstance with us walking through rushing water atop a washed-out bridge carrying weighted down bicycles. We were quite fortunate that there were no falls or injuries, or loss of goods while we waded the water made turbulent from the heavy rain.

We arrived in Walnut grove at 8:30pm having cycled about fifty miles for the day. We made camp in the town park too tired to prepare anything for dinner so we went without. A carnival was being setup in the park I wandered over to the commotion and met one of the carney workers. He offered me a beer, which I accepted, and we conversed for a time then I bid him good evening and bedded down for the night.

Tuesday, July 17, 1979

We did not leave Walnut Grove before noontime cycling to Greenfield in a few hours taking a break in town. Craig spoke to a local who informed him we were only thirty miles from the Kansas border. Our group took to our bicycles and pedaled sixteen miles to Golden City the last town in Missouri before crossing into Kansas. Those sixteen miles covered mostly flat road and the aches in my calves seem to dissipate as I cycled the evenly smooth pavement. At last, I traveled a road as I imagined would appear throughout Kansas and felt happy riding my Schwinn on a day with no rain.

In Golden City we learned that Pittsburgh, the Kansas border town was another thirty-three miles enroute. My happiness waivered slightly as I assumed, even wished we were much closer than that. We decided to rest in town stopping at a restaurant on Main Street called Cookie's where they advertised the "Best Homemade Pies" presumably in Missouri. Our group of five rambled into Cookie's sat an ordered slices of all the pies on the menu from Crumb Apple to Strawberry-Rhubarb.

After three or four slices of pie John suggested that we camp in Golden City and make for Pittsburgh in the morning. The touring group agreed so I exited the restaurant momentarily to locate a pay phone and call Patti, not having spoken with her since Kentucky. I noticed a public pay phone across the street from Cookie's and walked over to make a collect call to Patti's house. Her mother answered the telephone informing me that Patti was in the hospital. She went into labor last night delivering a healthy baby boy at approximately 4:00am. I quickly hung-up the telephone receiver and placed a second call to the hospital to speak with the mother of my child.

My mind raced with questions about the future as I dialed the telephone. Was I going to abandon my son for adoption as planned? Could I make it to California from here with the little money I had left, and what was I going to do in California if I made it there? Did I have the remaining strength to bicycle through six more states and another mountain range on the TransAmerica trail? The switchboard at the hospital put me through to Patti charging the call to her room.

"Hi sweet lady," I greeted through the telephone receiver, "how are you doing?"

"I'm fine Jeff," she answered, "but very tired. Where are you now?"

"In Golden City, Missouri about thirty miles to the Kansas border. I called your house, and your mom told me you delivered a baby boy."

Patti's voice lifted with excitement, "Yes and he's so cute, his birth weight was seven pounds, six ounces. The nurse let me hold him and he's … he's just beautiful!"

I asked solemnly, "Is the Adoption Agency there?"

Yes, a woman from the agency is here," answered Patti, "she's in the room with me right now."

"Well, you can tell her the deal is off," I instructed as a big lump rose in my throat, "tell her that we are keeping our son."

"Oh Jeff," Patti exclaimed, "do you really mean it?"

"Yes, baby I mean it, we're going to keep him and raise him as husband and wife. I'll take a bus from Pittsburgh, Kansas to New York and make arrangements to have my folks pick me up in the city. I should be home in a few days, and we can move in with my parents, you, me and the baby. So, you can tell the Adoption Agency to leave … they are not taking our son!"

"Oh, thank you," Patti remarked weeping, "I love you so much."

"I love you too, sweet lady, I've got to go now, so …"

"Wait!" Patti interrupted, "What are we going to name our son?"

I thought a moment and responded, "I don't know … I really don't want to do this on a long-distance phone call. Okay, how about giving him a rhyming name like Toby, or Titus Tuthill?"

"No, those are silly," Patti remarked, "they sound like circus names. Let's name him after you, Jeff junior. We can call him JP for short."

"Nah sweet lady," I commented, I do not want to burden my son with junior after his name. On second thought JP may give the incentive to become wealthy, like JP Getty. Let's decide when I come home. I'm going to hang up now … goodbye sweet lady. I love you."

"I love you too. Goodbye Jeff, see you in a few days."

I hung up the telephone receiver and exited the phone booth in a bit of a daze crossed the street returning to Cookie's.

"Hey Jeff, how's Patti?" John queried and suggested, "Pull up a seat and have some more pie."

"Try the boysenberry, its really tart." John recommended, "Is there something wrong?"

"No, I'm fine," I sat and answered still in a daze, "and Patti's fine … she delivered a baby boy this morning." I did not order another slice.

"That's Great!" John exclaimed, "Congratulations Dad! So, what are you going to do?"

"Well, I am definitely quitting the bike trip. I'll cycle into Kansas and catch a bus back to New York City from there. I will call my folks and tell them what I'm doing, so they can pick me up when I arrive in a few days."

Craig, Stinky and Jingles also congratulated me on becoming a father and I treated them all to their choices of pie slices instead of cigars to celebrate. The celebration continued into the night, we made camp in the town park, Stinky and Jingles sprung for a couple of cases of beer. I proceeded to get plastered and, in my drunkenness, began to wonder about my decision.

Originally Patti and I agreed to place our newborn with an adoption agency and in return they would cover all the costs for the baby's delivery. Now that we decided to keep our son, we assumed the cost of his birth and I worried in my drunken stupor about facing those hospital bills with no health insurance. Suddenly, those casual plans made with Patti before the bike trip were windblown by our new reality ... we would be parents. When the news of my son's birth sparked through the telephone wires into my head like a bolt of lightning, the casual plans we made were shocked into oblivion.

Within an instant, as quickly as I said we were keeping our son the great bicycle adventure evaporated from my mind, replaced by thoughts of marriage to the woman I loved and raising our son in a legitimate family environment. As I drank beer and laughed with my fellow cyclists, deep inside I panicked with worry. I felt distressed about hospital costs, arranging my marriage, and affording a place of our own to live. Assuming the responsibilities of a husband and father scared me worse than a downhill run in the dark. I drank more beer in an effort to drown these maddening concerns and it eventually worked, as I fell out dead drunk in a very calm sleep.

CHAPTER IX

Going Home

Wednesday, July 18, 1979

We were hungover from the beer bash in honor of my son's birth and got a late start out of Golden City. It was midday before we packed up our gear and pedaled out of town on MO-126. It was a straight shot across the border on mostly flat roads making bicycling with a hangover slightly more bearable.

By late afternoon we crossed the border into Pittsburgh, Kansas and I stopped at the first phonebooth I saw to locate a bus station in the telephone directory. I found a Trailways Terminal listed on S. Broadway and by asking directions from local pedestrians it did not take me long to find the bus station. I purchased a bicycle shipping box at the station in Pittsburgh along with a one-way ticket to New York City and asked them for the estimated departure and arrival times.

They issued me the shipping box and the ticket with a destination of the Port Authority Terminal in NYC telling me that the total travel time was one day, twelve hours and five minutes. The departing time was 7:50pm and arrival in NYC was on Friday, July 20 at 7:55 in the morning. John helped me breakdown my bicycle and pack it into the shipping box. I left it at the bus terminal with my panniers and our group located a restaurant in town for one last dinner together.

Over dinner we talked about our experiences on the bicycle adventure, and we laughed a lot about the people we met along the way. Reminiscing the recent memories got so thick that you could swat at them like flies and still have more than enough to warm your heart. Eventually, the effects of the beer hangover were gone, and I did not know if it was our last meal together, or the joyful talk of remembrances that cleared my head. After dinner we departed the restaurant while dusk was settling over the town of Pittsburgh.

John decided that the group would try for Girard, Kansas, a mere fifteen miles away and a good place to make camp. I said goodbye to Stinky and Jingles who I rode with since the Mississippi River. I bade goodbye to Craig with a firm handshake and a smile. Craig rode a long way with John and myself we covered a lot of miles together since Wytheville, always a cheerful travel companion. Lastly, I said goodbye to John my childhood friend and biking buddy with whom I planned and prepared for the Bikecentennial trek. If not for John, I never would have journeyed on our bicycle adventure. I knew I would see John again, as he was from my hometown and my old neighborhood.

I stood before the Trailways Terminal watching my bicycle buddies pedal off into the west in the soft glow of the setting sun. I watched until I could no longer see them riding the flat road out of town then I used a phonebooth outside the terminal to call home. My parents knew my plans to come home, keep my baby boy and marry Patti. My Dad asked me when I was coming home and where he should pick me up? I informed him that I was arriving on a Trailways bus on Friday, July twentieth and he should pick me up 8:00am at the Port Authority terminal in NYC. I said goodbye, hung-up the phone receiver, turned into the terminal, sat and waited for my bus. I waited for one and one-half hours before my bus arrived to depart eastbound from Pittsburgh, Kansas. Before departing and just prior to boarding I handed my boxed bicycle to an attendant to be loaded into the luggage compartment beneath the passenger area of the bus and carried my panniers up the steps into the coach section.

The bus departed the terminal at precisely 7:50pm and we arrived at our first stop in Ft. Scott, Kansas at 8:30pm. The Trailways bus made some half-dozen momentary stops through Missouri, and I soon fell asleep watching road-edge scenery blurred into the oblivion of my dreams.

Thursday, July 19, 1979

The bus stopped in Des Moines, Iowa very early in the morning for a one and three-quarter hour layover allowing the passengers to disembark for a meal at the Trailways Rest Stop. The driver announced the extended stay and the time as we pulled up in front of the Stop's entrance, it was 3:50am. I filed off the bus with the rest of the passengers wiping the sleep from my eyes, keeping my ticket with me as instructed by the driver.

The Rest Stop featured a brightly lit dining area with a service line reminiscent of every school cafeteria ever visited. A variety of hot meals were being served by staff looking slightly more awake than the customers. I slid my cafeteria tray along the rails of the service line considering the proper meal at 4:00am, selecting scrambled eggs with sausage. A service woman stood behind the counter before a heated pan of scrambled eggs wielding a miniature shovel resembling an old coal shuttle. She scooped up a healthy portion of scrambled eggs dumping them onto a plate, tossed on three dried-out sausage links with a pair of tongs, and handed it to me.

I took a small glass of orange juice to accompany my shoveled eggs and dried breakfast sausage sliding my tray over to the cash register paying for the meal offered to Trailways transients in Des Moines. I sat by myself in the well-lit dining area to partake of shoveled eggs and sausage. The eggs were lukewarm and tasteless, and the sausage was mot much better than warmed and moistened hardtack rolled into breakfast links. I could not finish the poor excuse for breakfast but did drain the juice glass. At least the orange juice was passable, tasted like it was faux fresh.

After swallowing the last sip of orange juice, I rose from the table to return to the bus, and I remembered that Lazy Louie said he was originally from Iowa. I laughed to myself imagining that the shoveled eggs in Des Moines drove old Lazy Louie from I-oh-way to Miz-or-rah. I boarded the bus showing my ticket to the driver and found my seat where I left my panniers in the overhead compartment. The time was 5:15am.

The bus pulled away from the Rest Stop in Des Moines twenty minutes later with a few more passengers on board. One of the new arrivals sat across from me, a guy about my age with a full beard and moustache. He introduced himself as Charlie and told me he was traveling home to Chicago, Illinois. I got to talking with Charlie for a little while, but soon fell asleep again. I awoke when the bus pulled into Walcott Junction, Iowa at 8:30am for another rest stop. I did not feel much like eating anymore at the Trailways Rest Stops after sampling the shoveled eggs and sausage in Des Moines, so I settled for a cup of coffee to go and stretched my legs outside.

The Trailways bus departed Walcott Junction at 9:15am with the sun shining brightly for a wake-up morning. I was thankful for the air conditioning on the bus and wondered how John, Craig, Stinky and Jingles were fairing in Kansas along the TransAmerica trail. I suspected they would face little resistance cycling the mostly flat roads in the State and if they were lucky, they would catch some tail winds instead of the opposite. Yes, it should be easy going until they hit the Rockies in Colorado, at least they would have one State to cycle through without any mountains. I decided to definitely reunite with John after he returned from the Bikecentennial trip.

In contemplation of the planned bicycle trip I made with John, facing some nearly nonexistent roads and campsites along the way, I regretted not reaching Missoula, Montana to protest the negligent inaccuracy of their trail guides. I remembered grumbling along with John when we arrived at a suggested campsite at the end of a day's cycling to discover it no longer existed. We also cursed them on the occasions of dragging our bicycles across busted-up pavement for miles with no reference of road conditions in the unrevised guidebooks. There were a few reasons I wanted to stop by the Bikecentennial Headquarters in Missoula and give them a piece of my mind, alas I would not get that chance now. I wondered if John would make it that far and go to Bikecentennial to lodge a complaint? I hoped he would as their negligence to updating the trail information surely caused us aggravation along the way.

Friday, July 20, 1979

My bus pulled into the Port Authority Terminal in Manhattan at 7:55am and I exited for the street with my boxed bicycle and panniers exhausted from lack of sleep. Dad waited for me at the Terminal and helped me carry my things to his pick-up truck parked on 8th Avenue. We loaded my stuff in the back of the truck and departed the city heading for the Midtown Tunnel.

I told my father how glad I was to be home, looked forward to seeing Patti, and my new son. We were on the L.I.E. in no time at all and back in Amityville about one-hour after I arrived in NYC. Patti was home from the hospital with our baby boy, so I quickly shaved, showered, dressed in some fresh clothes, and walked the block down to Patti's to see her and my son. I could barely keep my feet on the ground as I walked briskly to her house from mine. I knocked on the front door and was invited in by Patti's mother. I walked in to find my beloved Patti nursing our son feeling humbled and proud simultaneously.

After I hung-up the phone in Golden City, Missouri, during the bus ride home from Pittsburgh, Kansas, and the ride from the Port Authority Terminal to Amityville I fostered doubts. I doubted my choice in quitting a little less than halfway to being different and return home to an unwed mother, a newborn son, no job, no prospects, a significant hospital bill, and one hundred and ten dollars to my name. My soul was torn between my decision to quit the bike trip, a father's pride and how to support my family. However, when I held my son in my arms feeling him tremble like a body caught in a chill and saw the shine of his beautiful blue eyes, I knew I made the correct decision and my doubts melted away in the warmth of a newborn son.

EPILOGUE

Regrettably, I never kept in touch with Craig, Stinky and Jingles and I have occasionally wondered about them over the years. I did see John upon his return from the Bikecentennial trip, but even lost touch with him over time as moving around easily makes strangers of old friends. It turned out that the touring group seemed to disband in Colorado, Stinky and Jingles apparently went back to Milwaukee, John quit the trip catching a bus to his sister's place in California and eventually found his way home to Amityville. According to John, Craig went on alone all the way to the coast of Oregon, but since we did not stay in touch, I have no confirmation that Craig completed the trip.

I imagine that many of the thousands or tens of thousands cycling the TransAmerica trail year after year finish the trip. However, it seems that many, some unknown number of bicycle enthusiasts do not complete the journey like four out of five in our touring group. There can be many reasons for not finishing this arduous bicycle trek, psychological deterrents, physical inability, financial misjudgment, and simply being sick and tired of the damn mountain climbs in the sweltering heat or pouring rain. I like to think if my son was not born, I would have continued, but I believe I doubted my stamina for a host of reasons and the birth of my son rose to the top.

Patti and I named our son Jeffrey Paul Tuthill, Jr. or JP for short and he was made legitimate on September 29, 1979, when I married his mother. I collected Welfare for two months in New York State using this government-controlled benefit to pay Patti and JP's medical expenses for my son's birthday. Getting on Welfare was another one of those degrading episodes in my life, equivalent to the demoralization of swearing under oath to be a knowing negligent father for child adoption purposes, and I cannot say which moment made me feel worse.

By October of 1979 I obtained fulltime employment with Underwriters Laboratories in Melville, NY, my first adult profession and by 1980 we were living in our own apartment in Amity Harbor. As I buckled down to earn a living for my family, I dreamt of someday finishing the bicycle trip on the TransAmerica trail, but realized deep-down I would never get the chance. The ambition to complete the bicycle trek faded over the years into a vague notion until my adventure in 79' rests as a fond memory.

Patti and I moved from Amity Harbor on Long Island to Nashua, New Hampshire and eventually bought a house in our New England town. I fell on hard times again working temporary jobs, Patti and I separated and eventually divorced, we were married for sixteen years. I met a pretty, kind, but volatile Japanese waitress and we formed a relationship living together for one year. Patti was out of my life and Mitsuko arrived to transform me. Mitsu brought me good fortune as I received fulltime employment and eventual transfer to California. Mitsuko and I married December 12, 1996.

In my midlife I even considered making the bicycle trip with more comfort in mind, as my body became less accustom to camping outdoors. In the late nineties I resided in the Silicon Valley of California and considered that area to be a good starting point to undertake an eastbound bicycle trek pedaling back to Pittsburgh, Kansas, but staying this time in motels along the way. I could use my laptop instead of the black notebook to write my journal assuming I would have power availability at the motels. Yet, it was not to be, my considerations faded into dreams and I was destined to remain halfway to different.

After being laid-off from my career in California at the end of 2001 as a result of nationwide cutbacks from the 9-11 tragedy, I scrambled for work, attending career employment training, and sending out multiple resumes. The hopes of completing the cross-country bicycle trip finally and irretrievably died when we were still living in San Jose, CA and I went into survivor mode from loss of my job. After some discussion with Mitsu, we decided to relocate to Okinawa, Japan, my wife's birthplace.

Mitsu and I vacationed in Okinawa a few years in a row beginning in 1998, so it was not a spur of the moment decision to move there. We dearly love Okinawa and it truly is a tropical paradise with very little industrial presence, which can be a problem for a foreigner looking for career employment. Seeing how I was a foreigner (gaijin) in Japan and do not speak Japanese fluently, finding work in Okinawa became, let us say problematic.

Just before I was laid-off in California and right after 9-11-2001, Mitsu and I traveled to Okinawa. We attended the 3rd Worldwide Uchinanchu Festival — known simply as the Taikai — which is a four-day event. A festival that welcomes Okinawans from around the world to experience and celebrate Okinawa's rich culture, which happens every five years. We attended as part of the San Francisco (Kenjinkai) Okinawa Organization to participate in the festival.

I brought my resume with me, either in fear of losing my job, or not is unimportant as I carried copies with me just the same. I handed it out to the few English-speaking locals I met at the festival, and I am sure it was circulated around the small island. Sure enough, after a few months of losing work in California I began negotiating for a position in Okinawa to be contracted to the US Department of Defense Dependent Schools (DoDDS) via e-mail. I received an offer from an IT Contractor to DoDDS to manage their repair service for computer equipment at the DoDD Schools in Okinawa, Main-Land Japan, and South Korea. In February 2002 we moved from San Jose, CA to Mitsu's hometown of Nishihara, Okinawa, Japan.

We were happy living in Okinawa despite my lack of speaking or understanding the local language. We lived meager, yet enjoyable lives on our island of twelve hundred square miles, which at the time maintained a population of less than one million – three hundred thousand with ten percent of the land occupied by US Military bases. Still, Okinawa is considered one of the most peaceful places and touting the highest human longevity rate on the planet. The Okinawan, or Uchinanchu people are for the most part very hospitable certainly no less than those our touring group encountered on the TransAmerica trail.

I am retired now, living with Mitsu in a retirement community in Mesa, Arizona hoping to make the long trip to Okinawa one last time. It has been forty-four years since I experienced my bicycle adventure with John, Craig, Stinky and Jingles. JP is retired from the US Army after twenty years of service and we keep in touch though infrequently. His mother and my first wife, Patti lives somewhere in the southern United

States. I am not sure where she resides, exactly as we sadly have no contact with each other.

    I underwent a kidney transplant in August of 2021 and thankfully, I am doing well with my new kidney. So, Mitsu's and my retired lives continue here in Arizona and the sweltering heat of the summers here remind me of the bicycle adventure long ago. When we pedaled in anguish up those steep mountain climbs, begging for a cool wind to dry the sweat from our bodies. Oddly, as much as one's life changes, physical and mental stimulations stir memories of long forgotten events. Such is it with me remembering my bicycle adventure and documenting the moments from my journal as Halfway to Different.

If you decide to attempt the TransAmerica Bicycle Trip, here are a few things to consider.

(1) **Contact Adventure Cycling Association** – www.adventurecycling.org, Mailing Address. Adventure Cycling Association 150 East Pine Street P.O. Box 8308 Missoula, MT 59802, Phones and Fax: 800) 755-2453 Toll-Free (800) 721-8719 Cyclosource Store Orders (800) 611-8687 Tours Department (406) 721-1776 in Montana (406) 721-8754 Fax. Let them help you plan your trip.

(2) **Purchase a good touring bicycle** (light and sturdy) with rear and front panniers, a bicycle tool kit, air pump and the most comfortable bicycle saddle you can find. Leather bicycle saddles are really good as they conform to your rearend.

(3) **Train for at least one month** before you attempt the TransAmerica bicycle trip and find as hilly a terrain as possible, the steeper the better.

(4) **Carry $1,000.00 - $2000.00** with you and/or a major credit card. Short of that and you will reduce your chances of completing the trip.

(5) **Do not overpack for the trip.** Bring only necessities like a sleeping bag, lightweight tent, camping lantern, lightweight camping stove, a few changes of clothes (1 pair of slacks and nice shirt is optional), windbreaker, rain poncho, swimsuit, towel and one week's worth of backpack food (freezedried food packets). I left out electronics, cell phone, tablet, etc., if you feel they are necessary bring them, but keeping them charged on the trail can be difficult. Target 25 lbs., or less for your bicycle panniers.

(6) **Consider mailing yourself care packages** containing food, clothing, and bicycle parts (bicycle tires, etc.) to various Post Offices along the route to reduce what you have to carry and reduce your expenses.

(7) **Bicycle repair shops** are few and far-in-between on the TransAmerica trail, definitely **carry spare tire spokes, tube patch kit, or spare tire tubes.**

(8) **Plan to stop at the Bike Surgeon in Carbondale, Illinois** for any major **repairs**, or **upgrades** to your **bicycle**.

(9) **Cycle safely**, have a good bicycle helmet and carry a florescent safety vest. Make sure you are outfitted with Chamois (padded) bike shorts, cycling shoes, and gloves for comfortable riding and avoid bicycling after dark.

(10) **Make Sure to Have Fun on Your Bicycle Adventure!**

www.ingramcontent.com/pod-product-compliance
Lightning Source LLC
LaVergne TN
LVHW010602070526
838199LV00063BA/5044